PERSONS, PRIVACY, AND FEELING
Essays in the Philosophy of Mind

PERSONS, PRIVACY, AND FEELING
Essays in the Philosophy of Mind

Edited by Dwight Van de Vate, Jr.

Memphis State University Press   Memphis

Preface

The chapters of this book were originally a series of articles in *The Southern Journal of Philosophy* entitled "Series: The Philosophy of Mind." They appeared as follows: the Introduction, "The Future of the Philosophy of Mind" by E. M. Adams and Chapter I, "The Privacy of Feelings" by Douglas Browning, in Volume 3, Number 1 (Spring, 1965), on pp. 38–44 and 45–56; Chapter II, "The Social Theory of Feelings" by Charles Hartshorne, in Volume 3, Number 2 (Summer, 1965), on pp. 87–93; Chapter III, "Privacy" by Donald F. Gustafson, in Volume 3, Number 3 (Fall, 1965), on pp. 140–146; Chapter IV, "The Sense of the Senses" by Erwin W. Straus, in Volume 3, Number 4 (Winter, 1965), on pp. 192–201; Chapter V, "Problems in the Philosophy of Mind" by Edward H. Madden, in Volume 4, No. 1 (Spring, 1966), on pp. 33–40; and finally, Chapter VI, "Strawson's Concept of a Person" by Dwight Van de Vate, Jr., in Volume VII, No. 1 (Spring, 1969), on pp. 9–24. Through an inadvertence Chapter VI did not bear the "Series" designation.

Before the first World War, philosophy in Great Britain and America (which tends to copy British philosophical fashions) was Hegelian and metaphysical. The war stimulated the anti-metaphysical reaction we associate with Bertrand Russell, G. E. Moore, Ludwig Wittgenstein's *Tractatus Logico-Philosophicus,* and the Logical Positivism epitomized by A. J. Ayer's *Language, Truth, and Logic.* Philosophers began to think of their discipline not as a source of truth equal in authority to religion and the natural sciences, but as an ancillary contribution to science. The philosopher's function, they now thought, is to assist the empirical scientist by debunking his metaphysical critics and by providing him (through the use of symbolic logic) with a uniquely lucid and efficient language, a language expressly designed for scientific purposes. Metaphysics they thought to bear the same relation to the new scientific philosophy that astrology bears to astronomy: it had become an outworn superstition.

A second World War brought second thoughts about this dismissal of metaphysics. Wittgenstein in his later philosophy and Gilbert Ryle in *The Concept of Mind* argued that the Positivistic techniques of the interwar period were insufficient either to clarify or to eliminate such familiar problems as whether one can be certain of the existence of other minds or how mind is related to matter. While they in turn dismissed these problems by other techniques, their doing so suggested that the problems are indeed respectable objects of philosophical concern. The result was, and is, a revival of metaphysics—to be sure, a most controversial revival. At the center of controversy is what we call "the philosophy of mind."

In planning our Series, we wanted to show how the problems of the nature of mind, body, self, persons, and consciousness are approached by contemporary philosophers from a variety of philosophical tendencies and perspectives. Our sampling is not complete—no sampling could be—and since our aim was originality, the authors speak for themselves, not for schools or groups. The diversity of points of view on a single set of problems testifies, we think, to the ubiquity and durability of the problems themselves.

Each chapter appears as originally written for the Series, except Chapter IV, which Professor Gustafson wished to revise. Because I was special editor for the Series, William B. Barton, Co-Editor of the *Journal*, insists that my name alone appear as editor of this book; however, his assistance has been invaluable. The authors and I also wish to thank Carroll R. Bowman, Gene G. James, and David A. Coomber for their assistance, and Michael DeArmey for preparing the index.

DWIGHT VAN DE VATE, JR.

Knoxville, Tennessee
July, 1969

Contents

PERSONS, PRIVACY, AND FEELING
Essays in the Philosophy of Mind

INTRODUCTION

The Future of the Philosophy of Mind

by E. M. Adams

I find it very difficult to say much about the future of the philosophy of mind other than to say that there will be one. Philosophy of mind is in no danger of fading away. Each generation, indeed each philosopher, must wrestle with the age-old perplexities about the mental. The development of an empirical scientific psychology, instead of replacing philosophy of mind, multiplies its problems and makes them more acute and demanding.

E. M. Adams was educated at the University of Richmond, Colgate-Rochester Divinity School, and Harvard (Ph.D., 1948). He has taught at Ohio University and the University of Southern California and is currently Professor of Philosophy at the University of North Carolina at Chapel Hill, where he was chairman of the Department of Philosophy from 1960–1965. He has been a member of the Council of the American Philosophical Association, Eastern Division, and has been president of the Southern Society for Philosophy and Psychology. He is the author of *Fundamentals of General Logic, Ethical Naturalism and the Modern World-View*, and editor of *Categorial Analysis and Commonsense Realism*, as well as contributor to a number of other books, encyclopedias, and journals.

Philosophy is centrally concerned with the truth, wisdom, or insight embodied in our conceptual schemes as such, especially that contained in their categorial structure. Philosophical inquiry is spurred on, as is thought in general, by oddities and apparent incongruities and inconsistencies. Psychology, as an empirical science, talks about the mental, the behavioral, and the personal in causal explanatory concepts which seem to be incompatible with our ordinary ways of talking about such matters in terms of logical, epistemic, and normative concepts. Furthermore, the carrying on of the scientific investigation itself requires that we talk about the activities of the investigating scientists in just these ordinary ways. Therefore, scientific psychology seems to demand that we talk about its subject matter in terms of two teams of concepts which appear to be incompatible with one another. Here is a prime example of philosophical perplexity for philosophy of mind.

Although I am confident that the future of this area of philosophical investigation is assured, I claim no foreknowledge of the form it will take. The best that I can do in this regard is to consider several basic questions in the philosophy of mind, point out how I think we have gone wrong on them in the past, and indicate something about how I think they might be dealt with in the future.

The three questions I shall discuss are: (1) What is it for something to be in one's mind? (2) How is one's mind, or the mental, in the world? and (3) How does the mind stand in relation to language and logic?

(1). What is it for something to be in one's mind?

In ordinary language, we say such things as "What do you have in mind?" "There has been nothing like it in my experience," "You were in my dream last night," "I will keep you in mind," "My mind went blank," "His mind is a vacuum," "Put it out of your mind," "There has been nothing like it in the memory of anyone now living," and the like.

These ways of talking support the philosophical claim that a mind is the kind of thing that has contents. But if we are not to be misled, we must be clear about what it is for something to be in one's mind.

It was here that the classical empiricists went wrong. They interpreted "being in the mind" much like being in space and time. The early empiricists, Locke for example, regarded events in space and time as producing effects in one's mind. These effects were thought of and talked about in terms of the concepts applied to events in the objective space-time world. They were regarded as occurrences which have relations among themselves as well as to their causes in objective space and time. The mind came to be conceived as a subjective replica of objective space and time. This line of thought naturally led to the rejection of the doctrine of abstract ideas. If only particulars can exist in objective space and time, then only particulars can exist in their subjective counterparts. There can be general terms in language but not general ideas in the mind.

There was a problem, of course, for those who thought this way about how events in the objective space-time world could have effects in the subjective space-time realm and how an effect in one's mind could be an idea of its cause. The picture analogy was invoked to illuminate these problems. It was said that subjective space, the mind, is like the space of a picture. It has its own contents which are caused, in the case of a photographic picture, by objects in physical space and the contents of the picture are said to be pictures of their causes by virtue of the fact they were both caused by and resemble them. Of course, the analogy allowed for pictures of pictures, or originals and reproductions, i.e., Hume's impressions and ideas.

This way of thinking had to break down. The space and contents of pictures are just as public as physical space and its contents. The two spaces come together so that, speaking commonsensically, the contents of the two can be directly compared. This is not so for the mind conceived as a subjective space-time continuum with contents in the manner of the objective space-time world.

This puzzle led Berkeley to reverse the analogy, but not without keeping much of what had already been wrought by interpreting the mind as a subjective replica of physical space and time. He said for something to be is for it to be perceived. But the empiricists had already concluded, and Berkeley never rejected this, that for something to be perceived is for it to occur in one's field of consciousness. So public space-time was conceived as the mind of God. Presumably, for Berkeley there is not as much perplexity about how two minds can be together and share contents as there is about how a subjective space-time world can be related to an objective physical space-time realm. But for some who think of mind in this way there is as much absurdity in talking about a genuine plurality of minds as there would be in talking about a plurality of physical space-time worlds. They have argued that consciousness must have the unity that has been claimed traditionally for the space-time continuum, and that the apparent plurality of minds is simply a provincial fragmentation of the one all encompassing mind, a fragmentation which some have thought could be overcome and unity regained in the universal mind.

I have tried to indicate in this overly simplified way some of the consequences of attempting to clarify what it is for something to be in one's mind by thinking of it as analogous with something's being in space and time, namely, denial of abstract ideas, problem about the external world and its relationship to one's mind, problem about the plurality of minds. There are others which we need not bother to mention. It is widely acknowledged that this way of thinking about what it is for something to be in one's mind leads to distortion and error in the philosophy of mind.

We are still in need of an illuminating account of what it is for something to be in one's mind. A great deal of work has been done toward demolishing certain theories which were attempts to deal with this problem. But most of the constructive work in the empiricist tradition in recent years has tended to bypass this issue. It has concentrated more upon our next problem.

(2). How is the mind, or the mental, in the world?

We have already noted something of the difficulties involved in trying to locate a mind in the world when it is conceived as a subjective replica of the space-time continuum. So conceived, it is itself a world in which things are located and this is not the kind of thing which can be located in the world. Thus it is not surprising that some have spoken of a mind as immaterial, as having no location in space, and as eternal, as having no location in time. But even within this mode of thought there is a problem about what it is for a mind to be and in what kind of world it has location. This is especially problematic if we admit a space-time world as the matrix in which physical objects are located and also admit a plurality of minds. Spinoza's bold double aspect theory of one world or substance was an attempt to render these matters intelligible. The idealistic denial of an independent space-time world and the plurality of minds in favor of a universal mind which may be fragmented in self-consciousness was also an attempt to deal with these puzzles.

All the problems and views about the mind we have considered so far may be said to arise from taking a first person approach. From within this point of view, the mind is

seen as distinct from the world. Everything that one en-
counters, experiences, or thinks about is in some sense in
one's mind. But one marks a distinction within the things
in one's mind. Some are taken to be in one's mind only, while
others are taken to be both in one's mind and to have an independent existence. The world is the matrix in which something is located in its independent existence. If one admits
that only the contents of mind which could be contents of
sensory perception have independent existence, and if these
are interpreted in a commonsensical way, his world is the
space-time continuum in which physical objects are located.
If one admits that the contents of conceptual thought have
independent existence in a straightforward way, one's world
must embrace a dimension of logical space in which concepts
or platonic forms can be located in their independent existence. This, of course, creates a problem about how a platonic heaven is related to the space-time world and how they
together can form one world. The very concept of world demands unity in the manner in which our concepts of space
and time do.

While the first person approach leads us to think of the
world as distinct from the mind, it leads us to think of the
mind as a kind of world itself, as a field or matrix in which
"things" are located. We talk about things occurring or existing in it. Now it does not make sense to talk about the
world's existing, for to do so there would have to be another
world, a peculiar one, in which worlds could be located. A
world is not a substance, and the two concepts should not
be confused. Those who have talked about the existence of
the world and have sought an explanation of it in terms of
foreign agents have confused the concept of a world with
the concept of a substance. Even Spinoza, although he does
not appeal to agents outside the world, is guilty of this confusion. In spite of the similarities between the logical be-

havior of the concepts of mind and world, there are considerations which incline us to think of minds as substances and as existing. The greatest impetus in this direction is the fact that we have to talk, at least at the commonsense level, about a plurality of minds. But the very logic of the concept of mind in relation to that of the world, when viewed from the first person approach, makes talk about a mind's being located in the world quite puzzling and highly problematic.

One does, of course, locate one's body in the objective space-time world and there are peculiar reasons why it is regarded as uniquely one's own. Thus one is tempted to say that one's body is a kind of isthmus between two worlds, and that the isthmus provides a way of locating the subjective world, if not in the objective space-time world, at least relatively to something, namely, one's body, that is located in it. Accordingly, when we talk about other minds, we locate them relatively to their bodies in the objective world.

Dissatisfaction with these ways of talking and their consequences has led many to shift from the first person perspective and to restrict themselves to the observational approach and to the concepts which can be rendered intelligible in terms of the contents of such experiences. This gives rise to behaviorism. Mental concepts are regarded as delineating according to noticeable similarities and differences among objects located in the objective space-time world. Within this approach there can be no puzzle about how mind or the mental is in the world, for the concepts can have application to only that which is already located in the objective world in a perfectly straightforward way.

We should notice, however, that the shift by which this simplicity has been achieved is more than merely a shift from a first person approach to an objective approach which develops mental concepts from noting similarities and differences in the objective order. It is a shift from "mind" as an a priori categorial concept to "mind" as an empirical concept. As an a priori concept it belongs in the same set as "world", "space", "time", and the like, concepts which are of or about the conditions which make knowledge of objects in the world possible. As an observational concept, "mind", or the team of mental concepts, simply apply to objects located in the world.

But perhaps there is still a confusion. I have spoken of the first person approach as over against the observational perspective as though this distinction parallels the distinction between "mind" as an a priori and as an empirical concept. This would be an error, for mental concepts do have an empirical status from within the first person approach. Gilbert Ryle's behavioristic philosophy of mind, for example, differs from the positivistic variety of behaviorism precisely in that it analyzes the empirical use of mentalistic language in ordinary life situations where people are involved as agents in community life. They confront each other as people, participating in and sharing or opposing one another's views, hopes, plans and actions. Thus, the personal perspective may be regarded as a generalization of the first person approach. This gives rise to quite a different analysis of mental concepts from what is possible from within the perspective of positivistically purified scientific observation. But it still does philosophy of mind by an analysis of only empirical uses of mentalistic concepts. It fails to consider "mind" as an a priori category concerning the necessary conditions for there being knowledge of anything. It is this aspect of the matter which generates most of the problems, especially those concerning how the mind is in the world.

(3). How does the mind stand in relation to language and logic?

Two movements in modern thought have tended to separate mind from language and logic. The attempt to develop an empirical science of the mental, both on a phenomenological and a behavioral basis, led to a desemanticizing and delogicizing of the mental in order to make it an appropriate subject matter for empirical scientific description and explanation. At the same time language and logic were depsychologicized in order to get a proper subject matter for semantics and logic.

One consequence of this bifurcation, or perhaps its cause, we cannot be sure of the priority, was the conception of the mental on the basis of physicalistic models. This includes conception of what it is for something to be in one's mind after the model of something's being in the space-time continuum as well as the conceptual placing of the mental in the world of objects as a form of interaction, subject to scientific study simply as another form of observable relationship among things. Another consequence was the transference of many of the perplexities about mind to language. Note Wittgenstein's puzzles in the *Tractatus*. He was bothered because language could not be made simply an object among others. It could not be located in the world. Of course, there is a sense in which we can do empirical studies of language, but such studies are not exhaustive and may be misleading for the philosopher. There are problems which must be left untouched by this approach. Those today who look to scientific linguists to solve the philosopher's problems about language are just as confused and misled as their predecessors who looked to scientific psychology to solve their problems in the philosophy of mind. Neither is a philosophical analysis of the empirical linguist's talk about language sufficient, and for the same reason that philosophy of mind cannot be restricted to an analysis of the language of empirical psychology. The philosopher has a job to do with language directly just as he does with mind. He is concerned, as Strawson would contend, with the transcendental conditions of a language, the necessary conditions for reference, statement-making, and the like. These are not unlike the classical a priori problems in the philosophy of mind.

Pragmatists, both the classical and the linguistic varieties, attempt to narrow the gap between the semantic and the logical on one hand and the psychological or behavioral on the other, but they tend to do it at the expense of the semantic and the logical, although not as much so as they think. What they have not fully realized is that they have resemanticized and relogicized the mental and the behavioral in their ways of talking about them.

This seems to me to be in the right direction. Mind and language are not to be thought of separately. Depsychologized language as the subject of semantic and logical studies is at best an abstraction from the mental. In like manner, the mental or the behavioral, as occurrences subject to scientific observation and description in a positivistically purified sense, is also an abstraction. Both seem to be abstractions which distort and mislocate their subject-matter, for it has to be conceived as both aspects taken together, however embarrassing this fact may be. The mind, not the printed book, is the place where the logical and the occurrent, the semantic and the existent meet. We must insist on talking about the mental in terms of its own unique, indigenous concepts.

Elsewhere I have suggested that if we must use a model in attempting to elucidate the mental, perhaps the best one is that of an automatic or animated language which does all the things a person can normally do with a language. The appropriateness of the analogy is indicated by the fact that we can reverse the process and illuminate what a language is in terms of a mind. They are so closely related that one is tempted to say that mind is not merely somewhat like what a genuinely self-functioning language would be, but that a mind, at least in its more highly developed form, actually is just such a thing. The full team of semantic and logical concepts which apply to language apply also to the mental. In fact, language apart from being used by a mind to question, to make statements, to instruct, to command, etc., cannot be spoken of in semantic and logical terms at all. It is a mind or a person who means in the various modes of referring, asserting, questioning, prescribing, and it is the perceptions, thoughts, statements, desires, plans, and actions of people that are consistent or inconsistent. To desemanticize and to delogicize the mental is to dementalize it. And to depsychologize the semantic and the logical is to rarefy an abstraction. The fact that mental states lend themselves to linguistic expression through physical media, especially in written form, invites us to think that the abstraction of the semantic from the mental is in fact a separation. But the written form means nothing except insofar as it is used or taken to mean something by a mind.

In light of these considerations, I suggest that insights from philosophy of language will be helpful in the philosophy of mind. In fact, it is an error to separate the two. The philosophy of language rightly understood is philosophy of mind.

Let us now return to our first two questions. If I am right about the relation of mind to the semantic and the logical, what light does this shed on what it is for something to be in one's mind and how a mind is in the world?

In the area of language we talk about something's being in a newspaper, in a report, in a book; a character or an occurrence being in a play or a novel; the conclusion of a deductive argument's being in the conjunction of its premises; something's being in a given class, and the like. It is here, I suggest, that we may find an illuminating analogue of what it is for something to be in one's mind. In fact, it seems to me that we can simply say that things are in one's mind as semantic objects, as things meant in some mode of meaning. This is as true in dreams, imagination, memory, perception, desire, feeling, and the like as it is in the more abstract forms of thoughts, beliefs, plans, etc. Things are semantically in the mind and existentially in the world. What is in the mind may or may not be in the world just as what is in a book may or may not be in the world. However, what is in a knowing state of mind is also in the world. On this basis we are inclined to say that mind is like a book rather than a subjective replica of space and time.

On this approach, the problem about how a mind is in the world is not quite as perplexing as it is from the point of view which conceives the mind on the basis of physicalistic models. The body, especially the brain, is like the physical aspects of the book, and like the book, the neurological occurrences have a semantic and logical dimension as well. The language most appropriate for reporting and describing the psychological is that of indirect statements which indicate the mode of the semantic (I think that . . ., I plan to . . ., I believe that . . . , I desire to . . . , I fear that . . . , I hope that . . . , etc.) as well as the semantic object expressed in the "that" clause.

But this way of considering the matter does not solve all the problems. The physical basis of the mental cannot be simply in the world as physical states and events subject to only physical causation. The fact that a mind has certain beliefs and assumptions and that these beliefs and assumptions have certain logical relationships to certain other propositions must have something to do with the fact that one comes to believe the latter propositions. Therefore, the logical relationships in the mental must have something to do with the occurrence of the neurological events which constitute the physical base of the new beliefs. Therefore, not only the causality of the mental but also that of the neurological must be unique. The semantic and the logical, although not in space and time in one sense, are tied in with the spatial and the temporal through neurological events and influence them causally in a peculiar way.

It seems that our concepts in this area are unique and cannot be clarified by reduction to those of any other area. We simply have to conceive the world in a sufficiently rich way to make room in our conceptual system for these peculiarities. The philosophical perplexities we feel about the mental are largely functions of an impoverished categorial framework in terms of which we insist on interpreting the world. If we would only give ourselves a little more categorial room we would not feel so many intellectual cramps in the philosophy of mind.

I

The Privacy of Feelings

by Douglas Browning

A dominant theme of Western philosophical tradition has been the doctrine that all matters of fact are in principle subject to exhaustive cognitive or experiential survey. One consequence of this position is that the possibility of unalterable opacities, closures, or retractions in nature is denied. Against this view the greatest threat has been thought to be, and I think rightly so, the purported fact of the impenetrability of the person. More specifically, the problems of establishing the existence of other minds and determining whether the affairs of man's mental life may be properly described as private have continually arisen in the course of Western thought with a singular urgency and insistency. It

Douglas Browning was educated at The University of Texas (Ph.D., 1958), and is currently Professor of Philosophy at the University of Miami. Formerly secretary and currently a member of the Council of the Southern Society for Philosophy and Psychology, he is the author of *Act and Agent* and editor of *Philosophers of Process*.

is the last of these problems, namely, the problem of privacy, to which I wish to return once more.

To begin, I must delimit my field. I shall not discuss the problem of the privacy of human experiences in general but only the problem of the privacy of those affairs of mind commonly referred to as feelings. Even this is too large a topic, but I think a profitable beginning may be made. My procedure shall be as follows. I shall first attempt to untangle the issues surrounding the problem of privacy so far as they are relevant to human feelings. I shall then turn to an all too brief but I hope not too simplistic analysis of the nature of feeling. Finally, I shall return to a consideration of the controversies concerning privacy and, armed with some conclusions about what feelings are, make certain suggestions towards the solution of some of them.

I. The Concept of Privacy

In regard to the many disputes concerning the privacy or inaccessibility to another of a person's feelings it is not always clear what is being asserted and what is being denied. The following doctrines should be distinguished.

(1). The doctrine of the *ownership* of feeling. Every feeling has a feeler. Every statement of the occurrence (or fact) of a feeling entails a statement that some feeler had that feeling. The concept of *having* is left unanalyzed here.

(2). The doctrine of the *particularity* of feeling. A feeling is a particular, not a universal or a disposition.

(3). The doctrine of the *occurrent nature* of feeling. A feeling is an event or an occurrence. This means that (a) it has a definite place in some determinate chronology (perhaps that of a person or a feeler, if the doctrine of ownership is assumed) and (b) it has a qualitative temporal extensity, i.e., it is a datum which fills up a determinate temporal region. The particularity of feeling is assumed.

(4). The doctrine of the *qualitative uniqueness* of feeling. Every feeling is qualitatively unique. Any feeling may be said to be qualitatively unique to the extent that it is novel and is not repeated in its qualitative character.

(5). The doctrine of the *unsharability* of feeling. A feeling cannot be experienced by more than one feeler at a time. This unsharability may be held to be either logically or actually necessary.

(6). The doctrine of the *independence* of feeling. A feeling is to some extent free from necessary relationship to outward events. Contrariwise, a feeling may be said to be dependently related to outward correlates to the extent that a necessary relation obtains between them. The class of outward events comprises both physical events (other than experiences, if indeed experiences can be construed as physical), such as those occurring in or around the feeler's body or behavior, and the experiences of others, such as those which might occur in cases of co-consciousness.

Such dependence may be conceived as *logical* or *actual,* i.e., the necessity of the relevant relation may be logical necessity or actual necessity, and the respective correlates may be conceived as either *criteria* or *evidence* of the nature or occurrence of feelings.[1] Hence, independence may be conceived as the actual possibility of the absence of correlation or as merely its logical possibility.

Also, dependence, and hence independence, may be conceived as *complete* or *partial.* One who maintains a doctrine of complete dependence must hold that every feeling is necessarily related, wholly and in detail, to some set of distinctive and specifiable outward events. Partial dependence may be said to hold whenever a necessary relation obtains be-

[1] It is to be noticed that this formulation avoids the use of 'signs' and 'symptoms' and the distinctive sense of 'physical' which are found so offensive by J. L. Austin in his *Philosophical Papers* (Oxford, 1961), pp. 75–7.

tween feelings and outward events either in part or in general, but not wholly and in detail. Hence, partial independence indicates that correlation is contingent either in some respects or in detail, though necessary in other respects or in general.

(7). The doctrine of the *epistemological prerogative* of the feeler. No evidence for the occurrence or nature of a feeling can be stronger than the honest testimony of the feeler. The doctrine of ownership is assumed.

(8). The doctrine of the *alien unknowability* of feeling. Any feeling had by one feeler either cannot be known to occur (assuming an occurrent nature) or cannot be known in nature by one who does not have it. The term 'known' must remain unanalyzed here, though it is to be distinguished from the unanalyzed 'having' of (1) above and 'experiencing', and it is to be identified with the sense of 'knowing that so and so is true,' whatever the sense of that is. The doctrine of ownership is presupposed.

(9). The doctrine of the *incorrigibility* of the feeler's judgment. A feeler cannot be mistaken concerning the nature and occurrence (assuming the occurrent nature of feelings) of his feelings. Obviously, the doctrine of ownership is assumed. Here, 'cannot be mistaken' means 'knows with certainty.' The latter phrase is wisely left unanalyzed here.

(10). The doctrine of the *incommunicability* of feeling. The feeler of a feeling cannot communicate that feeling to another. The doctrine of ownership is presupposed. The term 'communicate' in this formulation means 'voluntarily indicate to another in a fashion understandable to him by means of language, gesture, or other behavior.'

It is to be noted that communication, in this sense, is never inadvertent. This is so because it is initiated voluntarily and with the intention of so informing the other. It is also worth noting that, in order for the feeling to be communicated, the transaction need not be consummated by proper understanding on the part of the other so long as the proper understanding of the indication is actually possible for him. This use of 'communicate' accords with the sense of 'transmitting information' rather than 'making known to another.'

(11). The doctrine of the *inexpressibility* of feeling. The feeler of a feeling cannot express his feelings by any outward means—behavioral, gestural, or linguistic. The doctrine of ownership is presupposed. Incommunicability follows.

Understandability by another is no prerequisite for expressibility. Were one able to frame a private language which was necessarily unintelligible to another, he would still be able to express himself by its means. All that is required for expressibility is that the feeler be able to frame a consistent language for the description or naming of his feelings,[2] or that he intentionally or spontaneously develop a pattern of gestures, grimaces, or other behavior by means of which he can give vent to his feelings. Obviously, the expression which is denied in this doctrine is to be distinguished from the necessary correlation denied in the doctrine of independence. An expression of feeling is not a necessary effect nor a logical consequence. On the other hand, the expression is not necessarily voluntary, at least not in any common sense of that term. A scream is an involuntary expression of terror.

(12). The doctrine of the *personal nature* of feeling. A feeling is a particular which is owned by only one particular feeler.

When it is said that "your feelings are yours and mine are mine," it is this complex doctrine which is ordinarily being asserted. It should be observed that the doctrine of ownership is compatible with shared ownership and perhaps

[2] See "Immediacy, Privacy, and Ineffability," by Ramon M. Lemos, *Philosophy and Phenomenological Research*, June, 1965.

even with a non-particular (perhaps universal) character of feelings. The doctrine of personal nature, then, simply combines the doctrines of ownership, unsharability, particularity, and occurrent nature.

(13). The doctrine of the *seclusiveness* of feeling. A feeling is personal and independent. Complete seclusiveness would entail complete independence, but a feeling may be said to be seclusive in such and such a respect if it is partially independent in this respect. Also, it may be held that certain types of feelings are completely seclusive while other types are only partially seclusive or even lacking in seclusiveness altogether.

The doctrines of ownership, particularity, occurrent nature, unsharability, and independence combine to form the doctrine of seclusiveness. But this doctrine does not seem at first blush to rule out the possibility that such seclusive feelings are expressed or indeed communicated, and hence it does not appear to rule out alien knowability.[3]

(14). The doctrine of the *necessary secrecy* of feeling. A feeling is (at least in some respects) seclusive and incommunicable. Doctrines (10) and (13) are combined to form this view. Also, the truth of this doctrine would serve to establish, if I am not mistaken, the alien unknowability of feelings.

(15). The doctrine of *muteness* or necessary silence. A feeling is (at least in some respects) seclusive and inexpressible. A person is necessarily silent concerning his own feelings. Doctrines (11) and (13) are combined. Necessary secrecy and alien unknowability follow.

Our proliferation of doctrines may now be halted. These fifteen possibilities will be more than sufficient for our pur-

[3] Malcolm and Wittgenstein seem to argue that such privacy precludes linguistic expressibility and communication. Though I think this view mistaken, I shall not argue the matter here.

poses.[4] In fact, I will be concerned in what follows with maintaining only the doctrine of privacy in the sense of personal nature, and that only in certain respects. I will argue that this sense of privacy applies to some feelings in all respects, but not to all feelings in all respects. Since, as we have seen, the doctrine of personal nature presupposes the doctrines of ownership, particularity, occurrent nature, and unsharability, I shall have to set out in what follows precisely how I take these doctrines to apply to feelings and offer my reasons for assuming such application. But first we must consider the nature of feelings themselves.

II. Some Observations on the Nature of Feelings

By the term 'feelings' I wish to refer to such affairs of consciousness as anger, pain, pangs of nostalgia, and anxiety. Such matters are to be distinguished from such other experiences as sensations, imaginings, conceptions, choosings, and judgings. They are also to be distinguished from such other elements of the mental life as traits of personality and principles of character, which as dispositional or normative structures are not in fact matters of experience at all. Moreover, feelings cannot be identified with those very pervasive fields of human concern which exist across the boundaries of conscious/unconscious and occurrent/dispositional. I have in mind such complex structures as desire, enjoyment, taking pleasure in, finding distasteful, vanity, love, hate, pride, etc., all of which incorporate or may involve experiences, traits,

---

[4] So far as I can determine, the problem of the privacy of feelings in no wise presupposes or need even suggest the peculiar doctrine invented by Professor Gilbert Ryle in *The Concept of Mind* of "a windowless chamber, illuminated by a very peculiar sort of light into which a person has severely restricted peeping privileges." Until Professor Ryle invented this doctrine I had never heard of it, nor have I chanced upon it since. I do not find it either relevant or suggestive in regard to the dispute and so have not listed it here.

principles, and patterns of behavior, and all of these in respect to a more or less determinate range of appropriate contexts.

Feelings are often confused with such fields, due in the main to a similarity in the phrases we commonly use to name them. For example, we speak both of being angry and feeling angry, of being in love and feeling like we are in love. Clearly, being angry need not involve feeling angry and being in love need not involve feeling like one is in love, nor need feeling angry involve being angry and feeling like one is in love involve being in love, though it is obvious that a feeling is more likely to indicate involvement in a field than vice versa. It follows from these considerations that not only must we distinguish feelings from such fields, but we must also bluntly deny that feelings are no more than elements or parts which may be abstracted from them. It has sometimes been maintained that feelings necessarily get their names from the fields in which they play their roles. I think this is surely sometimes the case. The so-called feeling of love is no more, I take it, than the sort of feeling we commonly have when we find ourselves in love. The same is probably true of the supposed feelings of enjoyment (not joy!), vanity, and courage. But on the other hand, certain fields seem to get their names from the feelings which are generally associated with them. The feeling of anger is not a feeling like one has when he finds himself being angry. One does not feel like he is angry; he feels angry. However, the field of being angry would seem to be no more than the sort of field one generally finds himself in when he feels angry.

It would be most helpful here if we could hit upon a defining characteristic of feelings which would serve to set them off from other affairs of consciousness. But I do not know of any, nor am I hopeful that there is any to be found.

Rather, it would seem that the term 'feeling' is topographical merely, referring to a station on the map of the mind. We can do no better, I think, than (a) distinguish the area from its logical neighbors, such as fields and bodily sensations, and (b) indicate its own subdivisions and specific varieties.

Feelings fall into three natural groups, which may be called *stirrings, moods,* and *emotions.* Stirrings are such occurrences as pangs and "mental" aches, which are distinguishable from such bodily sensations as hurts, hunger pangs, "bodily" aches, pressures, itches, etc. by the fact that, though sometimes experienced vaguely in some part of the body as are bodily sensations, they are not, like the latter, experienced *as* characteristics of one's body. Stirrings seem bare occurrences, transient unattached casts of consciousness which flit through one's mental biography like momentary gusts of wind. Moods, such as yearning, dread, anxiety, melancholia, depression, and sourness, seem to be more pervasive and somewhat amorphous changes of the mental weather. Our names for varieties of moods are few, and for stirrings they are fewer. In contrast, the language of emotions is rich and subtle beyond compare. There are appetitive emotions (wantings, passions, feelings of effort, etc.), epistemic emotions (feelings of doubt about, feelings of confidence in, etc.), normative emotions (feelings of the fittingness of, feelings of obligation to, remorse about, etc.), alethic emotions (feelings of spontaneity in, feelings of being constrained from, etc.), aesthetic emotions, orientational emotions (pain at, fear of, anger at, grief about, warmth to, etc.), bodily emotions (hunger for, nausea at, etc.), and perhaps others.

Of all emotions two things seem to be true. First, each has an object to which it refers. Second, the emotion is not exhausted nor significantly characterized by its object. This can be seen in the fact that two different emotions may have the same object, as, for example, the same object may be regarded as favorable or as unfavorable. Indeed we tend to classify emotions, not by their objects, but by their distinctive regards for their objects. Perhaps there are appropriate objects of fear and anger, say, but we do not need to determine what they are in order to sort various feelings under the headings of fear and anger. The names of emotions commonly refer to characteristics of how such objects are felt, as the list above will bear out. I shall call this referential "how" the *regard* of a feeling; I shall call that which is regarded the *object*. An emotion is at the minimum a distinctive manner of regard for some determinate object.

Now stirrings and moods would seem to be exempt from this duality. A stirring, such as a sudden pang, appears as an occurrence which may serve as object for some second-order feeling directed towards it, such as delight or apprehension, but it does not appear, on the face of it at least, as a manner of regarding another object. Moods, such as anxiety or sourness, seem on the other hand to be pervasive fashions of regarding which lack determinate objects. This is how such feelings appear, and since a feeling is no other than an appearance in consciousness, this is how we must interpret them. Therefore, it is not misleading to say that one type, stirrings, occurs without regard, and the other, moods, occurs without determinate objects.[5]

Now, it is not my intention to become involved in the sorts of elaborate considerations which have exercised Brentano,

[5] Many philosophers, e. g., Brentano, J. N. Findlay, and Everett Hall have argued that every feeling, even simple pangs and yearnings, has an object. Hall's argument in *Our Knowledge of Fact and Value* seems to be that there are responses and effects appropriate to these states. This is itself a dubious assertion, I think, but anyhow it does not prove what it is supposed to prove. Such objective correlates are not objects to which these feelings are directed. The arguments of Brentano and Findlay appear even more strained.

Meinong, and Husserl concerning the nature of objects, but several crude points may be profitably made here about them. First, we may distinguish between an object per se, as that which is intended by the emotion or, rather, that to which it directs its regard, and a *datum,* as that presented content which serves either as a surrogate for the object or perhaps as the object itself. A second point is that certain feelings or other conscious events may be themselves objects of regards, e.g., I may painfully regard my anger at John or angrily regard my painful regard of my anger at John. I shall call a feeling a first-order feeling whenever either it has no object (stirrings and moods) or its object is not another feeling. A second-order feeling will have as its object, and as its datum if the feeling felt is present, a first-order feeling, and a third-order feeling will be the regard of a second-order feeling, and so on.

Generically considered, regards are more elusive than objects, for the obvious reason that conscious emotional concern is always directed to the object, whereas the regard is that through which the object is posed. To use a very limited metaphor, one does not ordinarily see the window glass through which he peers. Of course, one's gaze may fall upon the glass, and one's regard, at least in many cases, may fall upon regards. But then, unfortunately, the regard regarded is no longer a *mere* regard, but also and perhaps now altogether a datum. It is the regard as present unregarded regard which is elusive. Consideration of the regard in the role of datum of another regard can at best only be a clue to what is of superior interest here, viz., the structure of the regard in its role as regard. Still, the regard is experienced; that is to say, it is a piece of the total experience. It is not as though we must infer the existence and nature of regards. Having an emotion *is* experiencing a regard for an object. The difficulty in coming to grips with a regard, however, is real, and here is at least one place in philosophy where the consideration of untutored beliefs, everyday talk, and imaginative constructions could well prove a boon.

Suppose, then, we consider an imaginary case of telepathy. John is in pain and Philip finds this out by directly feeling John's pain. Let us ask: Does Philip's feeling of John's pain necessarily mean that Philip is in pain? Surely this is a problem concerning the nature of regards, of how Philip feels John's pain, and not concerning the nature of the object, for what is not disputed in the example is the fact that the object, and here even the datum, of Philip's feeling is identical with John's feeling. What this imaginary case suggests to us is that Philip's telepathic awareness of John's pain need not be thought of as a case of Philip being in pain. In other words, it makes clear that we can conceive the possibility of someone regarding the occurrence of pain without being in pain. But if this is conceivable, it is only so when the pain felt as datum is someone else's, for, after all, to feel one's own pain means at least that one is in pain.

And here, I think, we may receive some aid from ordinary usage. When one says "it was painful, but I really didn't feel it," he does not mean to deny that he was in pain. In fact he may say without contradiction, "I was in great pain, but I did not really feel it." If we ask him further what he means by the last phrase, he may very well reply that he "did not mind it" or that he refused to let it "get to him" or "get him down." This suggests distraction or inattentiveness, self-induced or otherwise, but no one would I think want to say that one can be distracted from or inattentive to that which he does not in fact experience.

So, though Philip's feeling of John's pain need not be a case of Philip being in pain, John's feeling of his own pain does necessarily involve John's being in pain.

There is, yet, another consequence that emerges. It is conceivable that Philip be so constituted that he cannot telepathically feel another's pain without being pained at what he feels. Then we would admit that, in this sense, Philip's feeling of John's pain is always and necessarily a case of Philip's being in pain. But this is a case of Philip's having a painful feeling of John's pain; it must be distinguished from his having John's pain. It is a second-order pain.

Hence, we must distinguish between the cases where a person

(i) feels pain without being in pain,
(ii) feels pain and is in pain,
(iii) feels pained at some object.

In the first and second cases, pain is the datum of feeling. In the second and third cases, pain somehow characterizes the regard. In the third case, the pain is a character of the regard in such a way that were its object itself a pain-datum (a rare case in fact), then there would be two pains. But in the second case, though there is a conjunction of feeling pain and being in pain, there is only one pain. To be in pain one need not regard his pain with pain.

These distinctions may be represented in the following sentence forms:

(1) P feels pain.
(2) P painfully feels pain.
(3) P feels pained at x.

Let us say that in (1) the pain is *nominal* only; in (2) it is *abverbial* as well; in (3) it is *verbal* (predicate adjectival actually) only.[6] What should be kept clearly in mind is that the abverbial function of pain cannot stand alone. There is no being in pain without a feeling of a pain-datum or a

[6] This terminology is to some extent a refinement of that introduced in a previous paper, "The Autonomy of the Philosophy of Mind," *Franciscan Studies*. Vol. 24, 1964. Case (1) collapses a distinction between 'P feels pain in his finger' and 'P feels his finger as painful.' The latter was there labeled adjectival; the former, nominal. Though I still accept the distinction as a suggestive one, I no longer accept the conclusion of a motivational importance of the adjectival. I now reserve that role for the abverbial.

feeling-pained. This inseparability of the adverbial function from either the nominal or the verbal is logical; on the other hand, the problem of whether the nominal can stand alone, as in (1), is factual. It must not be thought that the previous construction of a *logical* possibility through the help of imagination commits one to the acceptance of the *actual* possibility of a purely nominal functioning. I do not care to argue this issue of fact. However, it would at least appear to be logically impossible to have a nominal functioning of pain without someone being in pain, i.e., adverbially. Furthermore, and this is another point, the verbal functioning of pain is logically independent of any nominal functioning, for we do indeed view certain of our feelings or other objects in a pained way without making the pain itself an object, but the verbal functioning is logically inseparable from an adverbial functioning, for to be pained at something is surely one sure way of being in pain. And a curious fact follows from this. Since the verbal demands the adverbial but need not itself become a datum, i.e., function nominally in the process nor have a pain datum, it follows that the adverbiality in this case modifies the very same regard as is in verbal function. To express this another propositional skeleton is needed, which should replace (3) above:

(3′) P painfully feels pained at x.

Also, and finally, it is logically and actually possible for one to feel pain as a datum without regarding it in a pained way, as when one distractedly or masochistically considers his pains; and hence the nominal does not require the verbal.

The conclusions we have arrived at concerning pain may now be put as follows:

First, 'P painfully feels . . .' must always be completed by either 'pain' or 'pained at x.' (Adverbiality entails either a nominal or a verbal functioning in respect to the same person.)

Second, 'P feels pain' entails 'P or someone else "painfully feels" in respect to the pain felt by P.' (The nominal entails an adverbial functioning in respect to the original feeler.)

Third, 'P feels pained at x' entails 'P painfully feels pained at x.' (The verbal entails the adverbial in respect to the same feeler.)

Fourth, 'P feels pained at x' and 'P feels pain,' are logically independent. (The verbal and the nominal are not related by entailment.)

These conclusions are, I think, significant. For example, the second provides a possible key to the old problem of why having a pain is considered a good reason for engaging in acts of avoidance. The problem is staged by assuming that pain is a sense datum only, and therefore logically compatible with any regard upon it whatsoever. That this logical possibility is also actual is supported by pointing out that masochists sometimes regard their pains with delight and that all of us on occasion regard our pains with indifference. Now, there are two presuppositions in this view: first, that pain functions nominally only and is therefore complete in that role, and second, that reasons for acting are always a function of the regard for an object. This last point is however ambiguous, for a regard may be considered in respect to either its verbal or adverbial functioning. I would certainly endorse the view that the manner of a regard is, among other things, a practical appraisal of an object, an evaluation for the purposes of the agent's thinking and choosing, but I would want to limit this motivational import to the adverbial aspect.[7] And since the adverbial accompanies all original cases of the nominal functioning of pain (and

---

[7] If this is so, then Kurt Baier's statement that " 'I have a pain' . . . says two things: 'I have a sensation of a certain sort' and 'I dislike this sort of sensation," (*Australasian Journal of Philosophy*, May, 1962, p. 7.) is misleading. Instead of 'I have a sensation of a certain sort,' we should substitute 'I feel a sensation of hurt or I feel as a datum a first-order feeling of pain or I have a pained feeling toward some object.' Instead of 'I dislike this sort of sensation' (which is really no part of it), we must substitute 'I am painfully feeling whatever it is I do feel here.'

perhaps in actual fact, all cases whatsoever) and moreover all cases of the verbal functioning as well, then I would say that the experience of pain naturally carries with it its own practical appraisal. The nominal is independent in respect to the verbal, yes, but not in respect to the adverbial. This dependence is, I think, shown in the very cases of masochism and indifference cited against it, for even in these exceptional cases we seem to recognize that, whereas we do not regard the pain-datum in a pained way, our awareness of the pain carries with it *some* justification for choosing appropriate avoidance behavior.

Let us now see to what extent our four conclusions concerning pain can be generalized to apply to all feelings.

Consider first the emotions. In general, I should think, the varieties of emotion are primarily varieties of regard in respect to verbal functioning. My manner of regarding an object may be said to be characterized by anger at, fear of, straining towards, hunger for, etc. Also, it is clear that to feel angry at is to feel in anger, to feel afraid is to feel in fear, to strain towards is to feel oneself in effort, to feel hunger for is to feel hungry. We might express this adverbially: to feel angrily angry at, to feel fearfully afraid of, to feel effortfully striving towards, to feel hungrily hungry for. The quaintness of such locutions lies in their obvious redundance, for the adverbial function is implicitly carried in the verbal.

One consequence of these remarks is that as a rule the nominal function of an emotion is secondary, i.e., is a datum of a second-order feeling. Probably the only exceptions are pains and bodily emotions, if indeed these are exceptions. However, there are emotions upon which second-order emotions cannot be taken while they exist, i.e., which cannot serve as data. Black anger dissolves before its regard. This is not because making it a datum serves to destroy its adverbiality, but because the direction of a feeling upon it would be to provide for it a rival in consciousness, thereby curtailing part of its very nature, namely, its blind tendency to fill up the consciousness. The experience we have of such emotions is always experience of them as regards alone. Insofar as "introspection" is understood as a process of inspecting a conscious state as a datum, then we must conclude that such emotions cannot be introspected.

Still, it cannot be denied that whenever one's emotions do function nominally, the adverbial function is necessary. Again, the conceivability of Philip's telepathic feeling of John's anger without being himself (Philip) angry cannot be denied, though its actual possibility is highly dubious. Hence, in spite of many differences between pain and other emotions, similar conclusions concerning the interrelationships between the nominal, verbal, and adverbial functions follow.

First, the adverbiality of emotion presupposes either the verbal or the nominal.

Second, the nominal functioning of emotion presupposes an adverbial functioning in respect to the original feeler.

Third, the verbal functioning of emotion presupposes the adverbial in respect to the same feeler.

Fourth, the verbal and the nominal functioning of emotion are logically independent.

Stirrings and moods, however, break this pattern. They are both pure states, the first functioning in a datum-like fashion only and the second in a regard-like fashion only. Numerous emotions may be directed to stirrings as data, e.g., one may feel disgust at certain tremors which he interprets as brought on by cowardice. This example points up the fact that usually, perhaps always, the emotion is directed to the stirring as a sign of something or other, not to the stirring as such. Since a stirring functions nominally only, it cannot function adverbially or verbally. It makes no sense to say that one is pangful or that one is in a pang or that one is panged at something. Moreover, as nominally complete, stirrings are motivationally neutral in just the fashion pains are often erroneously thought to be. Pangs and mental aches are never in themselves good reasons for doing anything.

Moods are never good reasons for doing any particular thing either, for they are non-discriminatory in regard to objects. A mood, in the sense of the word I use here, is an organizing objectless regard. It is, however, part of the force of a mood that it is practically demanding, i.e., it is a feeling of something undone, of a need for something to be done. If you wish, it is in search of objects towards which it may take an appropriate practical stance. Well, I hardly think it is really any of these things. What I want to say is that a mood is adverbial as well as verbal. One is always *in* a mood. Indeed, the adverbial function is just as apparent in our language as is the verbal. This point is very important, for it reinforces the conclusion that verbal functioning always and necessarily presupposes adverbial functioning, but that nominal functioning does not necessarily (as in emotions telepathically felt) nor even in fact (as is stirrings) require adverbiality.

Stirrings and moods are experienced in different ways. Stirrings are data, introspectable. Moods are, when functioning as regards, nonintrospectable and hence elusive in precisely the sense previously discussed. Also, moods cannot easily be made objects of second-order feelings, for it is their pervasive organizing nature to function as the ways in which the regards of other feelings hold together. But with this cryptic remark, our discussion of feelings must end.

III. Some Conclusions

I now turn to the application of these remarks concerning the nature of feelings to the question of privacy. I remind you that, of the number of uses of the term 'privacy' which are current among philosophers, I have determined to confine myself in these final paragraphs largely to the doctrine of the personal nature of feelings, together with its conditions of ownership, particularity, occurrent nature, and unsharability. I shall, however, append a brief note concerning the issues of the independence and seclusiveness of feelings.

From our remarks in the previous section it must be abundantly clear that a feeling, whether an emotion or a mood or a stirring, is a particular occurrence. Though the object of an emotion may conceivably be a universal, the emotion as such is a particular case of a distinctive regard upon the object. Of course, particular cases of emotion may function as objects themselves, and stirrings seem always to so function, but in such cases the objects are themselves particular events with specifiable chronological and biographical locations. Stirrings are primitively datal, functioning as present objects of some sort of awareness. Moods would seem to be primitively regard-like occurrences, only with difficulty and rarely made into the data of other feelings. Yet in both of these cases, as well as in the case of emotions, the feeling must be understood as a qualitative temporal extensity filling up its special place in the biography of a feeler.

This last sentence brings us to our next point, viz., that in any account of the nature of feelings reference to a feeler is indispensable. However, this requirement must be interpreted differently in respect to the different varieties of feeling. For, it is only in connection with (1) the regard of a feeling and (2) the functioning of an object as a datum that the doctrine of ownership, namely, that every feeling must have a feeler, can be said to hold.

As to the first, the verbal character of a regard depicts a distinct point of view. It is how things look from here, i.e., from this topographical post where I am presently stationed. And this post must not be construed as a bare spatio-temporal region, although that is surely part of it, but as a determinate vantage defined by a determinate biography, character, and personality. Briefly, a feeling is thoroughly standpointed so long as it includes a regard. Of course, the existence of such a standpoint does not strictly entail the existence of a feeler, though the existence of a person at the proper topographical post whenever the case of regard occurs does seem to be presupposed. It is still not explained, in other words, why such a person need be called the *feeler* or exactly how such a feeler may be said to *have* the feeling. But the adverbial functioning of the regard, which always accompanies the verbal, would seem to supply this deficiency. Adverbiality is the requirement that someone be *in* the relevant state, whether it be pain, anger, anxiety, or whatever. Or, to put it another way, it is the requirement that someone painfully, angrily, anxiously, or in some other respect adverbially feel some way or other towards some object. Only one kind of thing can be in pain or painfully feel, and that is a feeler. I trust that this is obvious. Moreover, a feeler may be said to *have* his feelings, insofar as this is distinguished from merely experiencing them, by virtue of the fact that he is *in* them or adverbially participates in them. It follows that such feelings are not merely standpointed, by virtue of the adverbal functioning of their regards, but they are also owned, by virtue of the adverbial functioning of the selfsame regards. And these are truly two aspects of one thing; the person at the viewing station is none other than the feeler himself.

But, of course, this only accounts for moods and emotions, since stirrings cannot function either verbally or adverbially. Do stirrings require a feeler? And to this the answer seems to be that, insofar as they are data for other second-order feelings, they do require the existence of a regard upon them and hence presuppose the existence of a feeler, though the feeler does not of course "have" them in the manner in which he has the feeling of them. Furthermore, stirrings do exist only as data for some form of awareness, even if not always one involving feelings, and thus always presuppose an experiencer if not a feeler in the strictest sense.

We come now to the problem of whether a single feeling can be experienced by more than one feeler at the same time. The occurrent nature of a feeling would seem to preclude the possibility that the same feeling can be experienced by different feelers at different times. The following conclusions seem to hold. (1) The regards of emotions and moods, in their functioning as regards, are uniquely standpointed to the feeler, i.e., they are how that person feels the object, and hence cannot conceivably be experienced by others. (2) The verbal character of regards, when made the data of second-order feelings (i.e., when functioning nominally), and stirrings, as data of feelings, can conceivably be experienced telepathically by another at the same time they are experienced by the original feeler. (3) However, the adverbial functioning of regards cannot be made the datum of a second-order feeling by another, for that would require that one person feel, not the pain which another person happens to feel, but another's-being-in-pain. It would be for Philip to feel John's pain as John's, i.e., to be in John's pain. In summary, then, the verbal and adverbial functionings of feeling are thoroughly unsharable, whereas the nominal functioning may conceivably be experienced in common.[8]

I take it, then, that the doctrine of the thoroughly personal nature of feelings has been established in part. What

---

[8] A. J. Ayer's discussion of the possibilities of telepathy and co-consciousness in *The Concept of a Person* (London, 1963, pp. 65–7) overlooks this distinction.

is asserted is that emotions and moods are particular occurrences which in certain very important respects can be had
by only one feeler, namely, in those respects whereby they
function verbally or adverbially. Insofar as one is in fear or
afraid of something or insofar as one is in a mood or anxiety-
ridden, then no one else is allowed to partake of these feelings. To the extent that moods and emotions may be made
the data of second-order feelings they are, like all stirrings,
impersonal—not in fact, certainly, and not even perhaps in
the realm of actual possibility, but at least in the realm of
the purely logical.

There is, I think, one very interesting implication of these
conclusions for the question of the independence, and hence
the seclusiveness, of feelings. To discuss it in detail would,
I am afraid, require another lengthy essay. You will perhaps forgive the brevity of the following remarks.

It would appear, first of all, that the doctrine of the epistemological prerogative of the feeler, i.e., the doctrine that
the testimony of the feeler concerning his feelings has special authority, is a logical consequence of the fact that no
one, save the feeler himself, has experiential access to his
feelings in their entirety. I do not suggest that the personal
nature of feelings supports either the doctrine of incorrigibility or the doctrine of alien unknowability, i.e., it does not
indicate that the feeler generally *knows* his feelings any better or more clearly than another, but it does, I think, establish the natural prerogative of the feeler, i.e., it does indicate that wherever there is a conflict of knowledge-claims
concerning the nature of feelings between the feeler and
another the testimony of the feeler has an evidential priority.
But it would also appear, secondly, that the doctrine of epistemological prerogative is incompatible with the view that
there necessarily obtains a complete and detailed correlation of outward events with feelings, for if such correlation

were possible it would be equally possible to balance the feeler's testimony with outward evidence or criteria. It follows from these two considerations that some degree of the independence of feelings is required. The affairs of mind are at least partially seclusive, lacking perfect and detailed dependence upon behavioral and bodily conditions or consequents. It must also be remarked that the fact of the personal nature of feelings precludes even the slightest hope of obtaining straight-forward empirical evidence for the correlation of outward and mental events, for one side of the correlation, viz., the multiplicity of feelings and other states of consciousness, are simply not open to empirical observation. Even introspection appears impossible on any useful scale. At any rate, all empirical attempts to establish even partial correlation must beg at the door of the inviolate person and make do with whatever scraps of personal report may be tossed their way.

II

The Social Theory of Feelings[1]

by Charles Hartshorne

Dr. Browning has attempted a difficult task. The subtleties into which he is delving are, I suppose, inexhaustible by any set of clear and distinct ideas. I particularly ap-

Charles Hartshorne was educated at Harvard (Ph.D., 1923), taught for many years at The University of Chicago, then at Emory University, and is currently Ashbel Smith Professor of Philosophy at The University of Texas. He has been visiting, exchange, or Fulbright Professor at Stanford, the New School, Goethe University, Melbourne University, the University of Washington, Banaras Hindu University, and Kyoto University, as well as Terry Lecturer at Yale. He has received, among other honors, the Lecomte du Noüy Award, and has been president of the American Philosophical Association, Western Division, the Peirce Society, the Metaphysical Society of America, the Southern Society for the Philosophy of Religion, and the Southern Society for Philosophy and Psychology. Among his books are *The Logic of Perfection, The Divine Relativity,* and (with William Reese) *Philosophers Speak of God.* His most recent book is *A Natural Theology for Our Time.*

[1] Read (in part) to the Southern Society for Philosophy and Psychology, April 16, 1965, at Atlanta.

plaud his recognition of levels of feelings, the possibility of having feelings (he calls them "adverbial") about one's feelings and about the feelings of another. It is very true that, on the one hand, I can find the knowledge that I am feeling pain itself painful, and that I might, on the other hand, take masochistic pleasure in it. Or, a woman, eager to end her pregnancy by a birth, might take reasonable pleasure in the awareness that delivery pains were beginning. There are many nuances of such possibilities. The structure of feelings in an experience can be who knows how complicated. In my book on sensation I had occasion to discuss some of these matters.

It is my belief that the notion of a sheer disparity between sensation and feeling rests upon a crude analysis. Basically there is one feeling aspect of experiencing, with many dimensions of variability, such as intensity, location in phenomenal space, massiveness, red-green, yellow-blue, sweet-sour, pleasure-pain, and so on. What these all have in common is intuited quality, in the sense of Peirce's category of Firstness.

Concerning privacy: I hold the view that any event is logically dependent for its concrete quality upon its antecedent conditions, so that to know the event absolutely would be to know all that preceded it. It follows that an observer who had absolute knowledge of the subsequent state of affairs in an individual's body could know what he had just been feeling. However, since no human being could conceivably have absolute knowledge of any event, this general principle by itself tells us little about the privacy, for most human purposes, of human feelings.

Is Browning correct in arguing that a "regard" is unsharable? Here, too, we must distinguish the absolute from the relative or humanly feasible case. If A feels B's pain, there is one sense in which it is logically absurd to say that he feels it "as B feels it." For how B feels it represents, as Browning says, the total momentary standpoint of B, and if it also equally represented the total momentary standpoint of A, then A and B would be the same subject. But it does not follow, I think, that it is logically impossible for A to feel B's feeling as B's. Philip *could* feel John's being in pain. What is—with one exception—impossible being only that Philip could adequately, or without "abstractive" deficiency, feel Philip's total standpoint. The exception is if "Philip" stands for the ideal knower, God. For the ideal of experiencing or knowing is indeed to be able to have another's standpoint in its fullness (without abstractive deficiency) as datum for one's own standpoint. The point may be simply put thus: divine knowing is always simply more, in no respect less, than what it knows; all other knowing is always both more and less, for in knowing an object it both has and does not have that object. God's subjective forms, in Whitehead's useful terminology, are the only ones able to enjoy as their data or objective forms the subjective forms of other individuals in their full value. All other objectifications do less than justice to the subjectivity objectified. God can feel my entire feeling, not of course as his own entire feeling (for this it is not), but precisely as *my* entire feeling. And this is possible without qualification only because God is the sole knower whose capacity to assimilate variety and richness of feeling is unlimited. He is individuated only by inclusion, not at all by exclusion. All others are individuated partly by inclusion and partly by exclusion. This is so not because they are subjects, knowers, or experiencers, but because they are nondivine subjects, knowers, or experiencers. It is this which makes them creatures rather than the creator, or makes them surpassable and localized beings, not unsurpassable or ubiquitous.

In the foregoing I have indulged in somewhat paradoxical

language. I have said that nondivine knowers both "have and do not have" their objects, or that they objectify the subjectivities of others only with "abstractive deficiency" (Whitehead's "negative prehensions"). This is the old paradox of error, which so puzzled Plato and, long afterward, Josiah Royce. If we experience something, how can we fail to know what it is? If we do not experience it, how can we even talk about it, as we must to be mistaken about it?

Consider as paradigm case that of extremely short-run memory. I have just heard a sound, say a bird's song, and am now interpreting the sound. I am aware not only of the sound's just having taken place but of my having just heard it. Does this not mean that the "regard" with which I felt the situation is even now a datum for my memory? But my present total standpoint is already slightly different. So here, in this simple example, we have awareness of awareness, not just awareness of a previous object of awareness; and if this is possible, then by what logic can one prove the strict impossibility of A's feeling B's subjective form? And if you say, Ah, but *I now* am really the same subject or owner of feeling as the *I* of a moment ago, and so the total standpoint cannot be the same, the reply is obvious: it certainly cannot be altogether the same, for the previous remembered standpoint is now object of a remembering but not yet remembered standpoint. And if you say, Yes, but in the genetic unity of the person through time there is somehow provision for such assimilating of earlier standpoints as objects into ever slightly-new standpoints, you may then be asked, And how do you know that there may not be more or less similar forms of unity *between* persons by which it is possible for the standpoint of John to become the object for Philip? If, on the other hand, you hold that, even in immediate memory, it is not really the case that the total previous standpoint becomes object for a new total standpoint, I would like to know how you can then be aware at all of such a thing as a total standpoint. Browning tells us that black anger cannot be introspected. If introspection is taken as simultaneous with its datum, I agree. But then if black anger can also not be given in memory, why talk about something completely inaccessible even to the person himself? And it is not to be forgotten that, according to a variety of philosophers and psychologists who have considered the matter with some care, introspection as a genuine function is a way of using memory and is really retrospection.

I submit, therefore, that any theory which makes the total feeling, regard, or subjective form of another logically unsharable, incapable of becoming a datum, will by parity of reasoning make one's own total feeling or regard similarly inaccessible, and that any justification of the claim to know one's own subjective forms will by implication imply the logical possibility of knowing those of another.

However one may best express it, there seems to be a human mode of being aware, in one state of feeling, of one's own prior state of feeling; and it is not apparent what absolute principle of inaccessibility to another can be justified which would not render one's own access unintelligible. I am profoundly convinced that there is no such principle. Hinduism and Buddhism between them, especially combined with the analysis of Whitehead, seem to me to have settled this issue, so far as it ever could be settled. Neither self-identity nor otherness of persons is absolute. Both are relative.

The awareness, whether of one's own or of another's feeling (one's previous self being in some respects another), is in the human case deficient. It fails to do justice to the concreteness of the subjectivities that are being objectified. But to express this by simply denying that they can be objectified, that total standpoints can be in any fashion shared, is to imply that in no such standpoint could there be knowledge of any standpoint, and then the very concept lacks foundation. To avoid this fatal result, I think one needs to admit that the total standpoint of another can in principle be experienced, but (in all ordinary cases) only in such a way that it is not possessed in the ideal manner or without loss of vividness, hence of value. But in saying this, one is implying by contrast the notion of an ideal or absolute form of the possession of one total standpoint as datum for another which, consequently, is in the most absolute sense more inclusive or richer.

I wish now to consider a human example other than personal memory of the inclusion of one subjective form, or regard of a feeling, within another—of course not without loss of vividness. In the feeling of pain, some bodily process is involved (I believe, even in "stirring"). Moreover, in the phenomenon itself there is a duality. Suppose the pain is "in my toe." The point is not that the bodily process is precisely there in the toe; for perhaps there is a case of pain referral and the process is elsewhere in the body. It remains, however, a bodily process, and it is not identical with my awareness of the pain. For the pain is directly given as "there," more or less sharply localized, while my total awareness, including the pain among its data, is not "there," it does not have the identical localization. This is enough to establish a duality. The pain is not the same as my feeling, but is rather something I feel, and this feeling of mine embraces, but is somehow more than, the pain, and expresses my total momentary standpoint. So far as I can see, the various aspects of the phenomenon fall rather nicely into place if we say that what I am experiencing is not just my feeling of my feeling, my suffering of my suffering, but my suffering of a suffering which is not just mine, not just my subjective form but somehow an objective form, down there, "over against" me. Yet what is over against me as something there for me to feel, is itself also feeling, i.e., pain. The bodily process appears in the experience, if at all, only as painful. Take your choice: the process is wholly hidden behind or beneath the experience as its unexperienced cause, or the process is present, a datum experienced. In the first case you have in principle the sense-datum theory in its objectionable form. In the second, you should note that the process is experienced only as the occurrence of pain. But then there are two sufferings, mine, and my body's—and not my whole body's but that of some bodily part or parts. In the suffering—or sufferings, for the deficiency in the human mode of objectification might easily obscure the distinction—of some part or parts of my body I participate, and this participation is my pain as mine. I share the sufferings of certain cells, presumably nerve cells, or cells closely associated therewith. How natural then the explanation of self-flagellation. It becomes a very special case of sadism. Part of what is special about it is that any pleasure in pain belonging to one's own body is bound to be tinged with one's own suffering in a more concrete fashion than is pleasure in the pain of a hated enemy. For one cannot but participate in the cellular pains that one is aware of. Thus this form of sadism is also in part truly masochism.

I believe that all feeling is participatory and that the alleged truism, no subject can ever feel the feelings of another subject, is not merely contradictory, but contrary, to the correct statement: every subject at all times feels the feelings of some other subjects. At all times, except in dreamless sleep, a sentient organism shares in the weal and woe of its cellular or subcellular individuals. What is true in the "truism" are the following:

a) No subject other than God can adequately, or without loss of vividness or distinctness, feel the feelings of another (thus we do not distinctly intuit the cellular or subcellular individuals in their unique individualities) ;

b) no human person normally feels with any appreciable distinctness the feelings of other human persons.

That we can more definitely feel the feelings of our bodily constituents than the feeling of other people is not inexplicable. The body, or at least the nervous system, is just that assemblage of subhuman individuals or events direct participation in the feelings of which is most compatible with the human mode of experiencing. Direct and vivid participation in the feelings of other human beings, on the contrary, is bound to be more or less embarrassing, to say the least. It is like trying to make a symphony out of bits of Beethoven, bits of Bach, and so on. Each person has his emotional (and intellectual) style, and the various styles mix only with severe qualifications. But the individual styles of cells can be mixed together to form a supercellular individual style, this possibility being the essence of the mind-body relation. By analogy, this is how God can mix the styles of all individuals into his own superstyle. The presupposition, in both cases, is radical superiority in the more inclusive subject. But equals cannot mix without grave danger of loss of individual integrity. They must keep their respective "distances" or mutual externalities.

Although direct intuition is severely limited (telepathy being at best an exception, not the rule), yet the privacy of human feelings as a practical inaccessibility should not be exaggerated. I think Browning goes too far in the anti-Wittgenstein or anti-Ryle direction here. There is no good reason to be more than mildly skeptical of the analogy between human bodies and their associated experiences. If human experience participates in the bodily life and feeling, and if, conversely (generalizing the conception), the bodily members are in their inferior fashion sensitive to the human experiences (which therefore can "express" themselves in bodily behavior), and if God at least can directly intuit what is on both sides of the mind-body relations, then anyone who admits all this and still argues that we have no reason to infer comparable bodily situations and states from comparable human experiences is, so far as I can see, indulging in an irrational rejection of excellent evidence without knowing what better evidence the case logically admits of. Add the social and public functioning of language, and we have in the inference as good a specimen of empirical reasoning as one could want.

If I am asked how anyone could know the truth of the theory of feeling sketched above I reply, Ask rather how, if the theory were false, one could know that! Popper can hardly be thanked too much for emphasizing that the sterile attitude in intellectual work is to challenge a theorist to prove he is right. Who can really do that? Progress comes mainly from accepted challenges to prove ideas to be wrong. We have to put our trust in what, at a given time, has not been proved wrong, although effort has been made to disprove it. The first demand of a theory is not that it be provable as true but that, if it were wrong, there would be some hope of finding this out. For instance, a theory should not be so hopelessly vague that it could not even be definitely mistaken, but only useless.

My theory seems definite enough to afford some handles for criticism. But "We don't know it is true" is not much of a criticism. And I have shown that the theory has some power to illuminate phenomena. Also it has possible applications to physiology, at one extreme, and theology, at the other, by which it can be tested for its consistency or lack of it with other assumptions that may seem appropriate.

An important criterion of any theory is the extent to which it unifies otherwise unrelated phenomena and does so without lapsing into mere vagueness or ambiguity such as render the unification merely verbal. My theory unifies the mind-body relations in organisms with the relation of God to the universe; it unifies causality and the subject-object relation in experience (for the causes of feelings become also their data), it unifies memory and perception, which in many theories seem utterly disparate, it unifies self-identity and that spiritual unity between persons which all higher religions, in greater or less degree, emphasize.[2] It also unifies common sense and behavioristic science, by implying that if we know the differences between bodily states or actions, we will have in these the keys to individual mental differences, so far as they are humanly knowable, and it does this without implying the paradoxical notion of qualitative differences that are unknowable absolutely and in principle. For it holds that (a) God has absolute, while (b) we have relative, direct acquaintance with at least some such differences. If, for example, I feel both a headache and a stomachache, I can compare the quality of the two pains. What am I then doing? I am comparing the sufferings of two sets of bodily members, and comparing them by direct, even though deficiently distinct and vivid, inspection. Also, to explain what I mean by "deficiently" I can contrast our form of direct experiencing with the ideal or divine case. That a human being cannot make a similarly direct and definite comparison of his pain with that of another human being is only a relative not an absolute gap in the human capacity to know how the feelings of one subject may differ from those of another. For each of the cellular subjects in which one participates is as literally "other" than oneself as another human person. "Inclusion" is one relation, "identity" is another. (One of the common errors in philosophy is the confusion of all sorts of intimate relationships with sheer identity. The converse error is the

[2]See my "Ethics and the Assumption of Purely Private Pleasures," *The International Journal of Ethics*, 40, 1930, pp. 496–515.

confusion of all sorts of less intimate relations with the absolute opposite of identity. A person is indeed intimately united with himself as in earlier states, but still not simply and absolutely identical with himself as in these states. And two persons, even though two, are not for all that without aspects of intrinsic relationships uniting them.)

The chief question, perhaps, is whether the unification of otherwise disparate phenomena or ideas which the theory effects is paid for by too high a price in indefiniteness or ambiguity. I am sympathetic to criticism on that score. But I am impenitently cool to the kind of criticism which calls for perfectly coercive proofs or which charges that the theory is too pretty, sentimental, or imaginative to be taken seriously. I am confident that lack of imagination opens few doors in the house of philosophy—or in the house of science. And the tough-mindedness which is really cynicism, or verbal questioning of the basic animal faith in life, and therefore in its cosmic setting, which all of us embody in action whatever we say, is to me merely sentimentalism upside down. I hold that there is no ultimate distinction between living and taking life to be primarily good, only secondarily evil, and I think it is merely a more adequate way of saying this to affirm the primacy of love over hate and indifference. Moreover, the concept of "feeling of feeling," where the first feeling has a different feeler from the second, is to my mind part of the minimal import of the primacy of love in reality. And I believed this long before being told so by Whitehead. But no one has shown, to the same extent as he, the power of this concept to unify otherwise simply disparate phenomena and ideas. It is as immense an intellectual achievement as our century has to show.

Dr. Browning's objection to my view would probably not be that it is unproved, or too pretty to be true, but that it cannot express the meaning of agency, of action and the actor. (See his book, *Act and Agent*, University of Miami, 1964.) I can see some point in his treatment of agency, but only by taking his words in such a sense that they are compatible with my theory. The incompatibility which he believes obtains arises partly from giving connotations to his formulae which for me are arbitrary, unnecessary to the real virtues of his account, and partly from attributing connotations to the Buddhist-Whiteheadian process theory which are similarly arbitrary and unnecessary to that theory. And I should indeed be surprised if any theory comparable in unifying power and clarity, yet incompatible with the notion of feeling of feeling (as intrinsic relatedness of momentary standpoints or subjective forms to other such standpoints, some within, some without, the given personal sequence of experiences, or stream of awareness) could be constructed. The social account of immediate experience (that it is *always* the givenness of a psychical other) is not refuted in contemporary philosophizing. Rather it is essentially ignored. This is to me only one of the many examples of how difficult philosophy is, and how far we are from an adequate method of disciplining our prejudices—including the rather natural preference for playing it safe by resisting all departures from the banalities of ordinary practical wisdom, or the natural human tendency to overreact against the superstitious aspects of our spiritual traditions, or the natural preference for half truths, with their neat simplicity, over the subtle complexities of reality.

Feelings are relatively private, in that, humanly speaking, a man's own testimony is likely to be about the best we can get. Pains are indeed parts of the physical world, bodily processes, but parts which normally only one human subject directly experiences. However, this relative inaccessibility to others is no metaphysical absolute. God is totally exempt from it, in that he has perfect access to all feelings; in at least four ways human beings themselves are partially exempt from it, for (a) they are somehow aware of God, who is aware of them and their fellows; (b) they are aware of certain cellular feelings in a fashion analogous to the divine awareness of all feelings; (c) they are aware of past feelings of their own, the subjects or "owners" of which are not in an absolute sense identical with the present owners; (d) the social or public character of language about feelings is scarcely a distortion of the actual situation, since feelings and their bodily conditions and effects are too intimately united to make the "argument by analogy" seriously open to challenge. The foregoing is a less simple view than mere behaviorism, parallelism, or epiphenomenalism. It is, rather, a subtle form of interactionism. But crude simplicities have always had to be abandoned in the end. The criterion, Does it unify (genuinely, or without mere ambiguity or hopeless vagueness) is not the same as, Is it simple? The social theory is not simple, but it unifies as no other does.

III

Privacy

by Donald F. Gustafson

The association between 'private' and 'feeling' is no closer and no more intimate than that between 'private' and anything else with which it is associated. There is a use of 'private' as an adjective and contrast marker for a wide range of things or sorts of thing, including its occurrence in 'private property,' 'private estate,' 'private bill or act,' 'private conversation,' 'private assembly, meeting, club,' 'private house,' 'private ceremony, marriage,' 'private communication,' 'private affair, matter, business,' 'private person,' and 'private opinion.' In each of these uses and perhaps others besides, 'private' has the force of distinguishing or contrasting the role or status of what it qualifies with a different role or status of the thing it qualifies. 'Private' in these contrasts

Donald F. Gustafson was educated at The University of Texas (Ph.D., 1961), and is currently Associate Professor of Philosophy at the University of Colorado. He is the editor of *Essays in Philosophical Psychology* and the author of numerous articles.

does not have just one opposite. Depending on the type of thing it qualifies, any of the following may be its opposite: 'public,' 'social,' 'accessible,' 'shared,' 'corporate,' and other constructions than adjectives. Furthermore, these may have words other than 'private' as opposites, e.g. 'secret,' 'privileged,' 'confidential,' 'personal,' 'inaccessible,' and 'individual.' 'Private' belongs to the same family as these and its opposites belong to the family of which 'public' is only one member.

These I take to be some of the linguistic facts relevant to investigations of the association between 'private' and 'feeling' and the descriptive sense of 'private feeling.'

One thing should be clear from the outset. If we understand by 'a feeling' a *private* mental episode, object, or occurrence, or some private *thing* "before my consciousness," etc., then the expression 'a private feeling' represents a logical stutter.

One use of 'private' as in 'private property' is to mark off a certain property as that which belongs to, or is the property of, a particular individual. What is private in this sense depends on who has certain sorts of rights in regard to it— right of access, for instance. Some philosophers have said that there is a sense of 'experience' and of 'feeling' for which it is true that one and only one person has access to it. Perhaps in this way 'private' becomes associated with 'experience,' through 'access.'

It isn't clear that this is the sense of 'private' required for the philosophical doctrine of private feelings. For one thing, the present sense of 'private' is as a contrast marker; it occurs here as derived from what we may call the legal model. On that model what is private is a matter of rights, and rights which are transferable. The right of access is transferable and sharable. But in philosophical writings on this matter the private access to "a feeling" or a certain kind of "experience" isn't a matter of rights but of fact or of logic. The philosophical doctrine of privacy has it that one and only one person has access or can have access to a private experience. 'Private experience' is like a permanent, non-transferable condition; there is no question of rights here. And there is no question here of claiming or exercising one's rights, and therefore no question of an infringement or violation of one's rights.

So the use of 'private' in 'private feeling or experience' is different from its use in the legal model. In the latter there can be transfer and loss; but feelings and experiences are sufficiently unlike property and 'I' sufficiently unlike a name so that no light is gained in thinking of "I have a private experience" on the legal model. "I own the pain in my foot," if it makes any sense at all, is very different from "I own those shoes in the corner."

Consider another approach to the philosophical expression 'private feeling.' 'Private' contrasts with 'public.' The latter occurs not only in 'public property' but also in such constructions as 'public knowledge,' 'public information,' etc. Some opposites of 'public' in these expressions are 'secret,' 'privileged,' and 'confidential,' as in 'secret information,' 'privileged communication,' and 'confidential report.' Since 'private' also occurs in these constructions it becomes associated with 'secret,' 'privileged,' and 'confidential.' 'Private feeling' and 'private experience' are to be explained, therefore, by analogy with 'private, secret information,' 'private, privileged communication,' and 'private, confidential reports.' The trouble with this attempt to explain 'private experience' is that private conversations can be shared, while on the philosophical account in question experiences of the private variety cannot be shared, either as a matter of fact or of logic. Secrets can be told and confidences can be betrayed; on the philosophical view in question feelings and private experiences can't be shared and perhaps can't even be communicated. And it is a further question what secrets and the keeping of secrets could be if there were no ways at all of giving them up. This attempt to explain the use of 'private' in the philosophical doctrine of privacy fails too.

Wittgenstein considered an attempt such as the one above to give a sense to 'private' in the construction 'private sensation.' What he said there holds as well, I think, for feelings. "In what sense are my sensations *private*?—Well, only I can know whether I am really in pain; another person can only surmise it.—In one way this is wrong, and in another nonsense." (*Philosophical Investigations,* Paragraph 246.) It is simply false that no one ever knows whether or not another is in pain. And to use "I know that" as a preface to "I am in pain" is senseless, because having pains is not something one claims knowledge of, renounces any doubt concerning, and not something one has evidence for, or learns of, or could mistakenly assume, and not a fact that one could stumble upon or think that one had come across. My sufferings and pains are not open to the kinds of reconsiderations, appraisal, and possible grounds for doubt that my knowledge claims permit. To preface a typical avowal of pain with "I know that" would be to suggest that my suffering and pain does permit such considerations on my part; and that is nonsense. For a speaker of a language an expression of uncertainty or doubt as to whether or not he is in pain is senseless; doubt has no place in these circumstances. (Cf. PI 288) Hence a claim to certainty has no place either. Furthermore, "You know you are in pain" and "He knows he is in pain" are not ways of remarking on his achievement in the way of knowledge. If, then, it makes no sense to claim one knows that he is having a pain by saying "I know that I am in pain," then it follows that uses of "I know" in connection with "what can only be known by me" cannot be used to clarify the sense of "private" in the philosophical doctrine of privacy. "You know if you are in pain," on the other hand, might be used to explain the meaning of the word "pain" to someone. But here "know" has the force of excluding uncertainty in pain cases. This much of the grammar of "pain" is clear already, viz., that uncertainty is senseless or excluded. (Cf. PI 247) So Wittgenstein's remarks concerning knowledge and pain are meant to block an attempt to explain privacy in terms of what only one person can know.

There may be other ways to explain "private" as it occurs in the philosophical doctrine of privacy. We are tempted to say that sensations are private, that my pain is mine, belongs to no one else, and is therefore private. Wittgenstein examines this temptation in Remarks 248 through 255. He tries to show, I think, that a misunderstanding of some harmless truisms accounts for such a temptation. He asks us to consider "Sensations are private." This seems a perfectly true, straightforward thing to say. But the puzzle is the *sense* in which sensations are private; it doesn't satisfy this puzzlement to repeat that sensations are private. So long as we don't get a sense for "Sensations are private" itself we must remain suspicious about a philosophical doctrine whose description contains the phrase "private sensations."

Consider Wittgenstein's remark "The proposition 'Sensations are private' is comparable to: 'One plays patience by oneself'." (248) The question is: In respect of what feature(s) are these two comparable? No card game which requires or allows more than one player would be a game of patience. We don't call any such game "patience." We shouldn't think of denying "One plays patience by oneself," and of course we might use this sentence to correct a mistaken use of "patience." To deny it indicates that one doesn't understand it. These are some of the features in respect of which "Sensations are private" is said to be comparable to "One plays patience by oneself."

But the fact that no one should think to deny a proposition does not insure that anything can be learned from it. In the present case the propositions in question are grammatical propositions. They express certain limits or boundaries in our language, for instance, that "patience played by several persons" is either nonsense or ambiguous and that "He had the sensation in my toe, and I didn't feel it" and so on is senseless. Because no one will want to deny these remarks there must already be absent from our language certain forms of words. (Cf. PI 499-500) We agree in not calling anything a game of patience if two persons are playing it. Nor do we call something a sensation if it isn't private, if, for instance, it isn't something we could keep to ourselves. But again, this fact doesn't supply a sense for "private" in the philosophical doctrine of privacy; rather, it partly accounts for the fact that someone might not find the occurrence of the phrase "private sensation" particularly puzzling, since no one would think to deny "Sensations are private." However, once this feature of "Sensations are private" has been displayed, reference to "private sensations" should become puzzling. For what is that form of words supposed to mean? Why not just "sensation" instead of "private sensation?"

Obviously there are difficult problems connected with this point. Simply stated, the idea of numerical identity does not apply to sensations, feelings, thought, etc. At the same time, however, I think Wittgenstein implies that numerical identity fails to apply to sensations in rather different ways than in the case of feelings and thoughts. What I mean is this. "It just occurred to me that it is Friday" expresses a thought. It may well be true that both Smith and Jones should truthfully express the same thought. There is no further question whether their thoughts were exactly alike, though not numerically identical—like their wives, automobiles, shoes, or canaries. The same may be true of their feeling when first sighting something or other. But the case with sensations is not quite the same. Because sensations—such as pains, tickles, twitches, aches, burns and so on—are not mental events comparable, for instance, to thoughts, numerical identity is not *necessarily* excluded as in the case of thoughts. It can be imagined that two people should have the same pain, not in that both have pains of a certain description in the toe, but that they have a pain in a numerically identical place. Wittgenstein suggests Siamese twins as an example. (See PI 253 and *Blue Book*, p. 49) If A should suffer in, avow the pain in, seek treatment for, and treat tenderly B's finger, then while it would be inexplicable if true, it doesn't seem to be a logically impossible hypothesis that A has a pain in B's finger. If this should come to be a regular thing we would develop a rather full-bodied idea of the numerical identity of some sensations. If in addition to A's having a pain in B's finger, B should not suffer, we would have a use for A's remarking that "B has my pain in his finger."

One might object that these bizarre circumstances are impossible because absurd. I do not think this would be correct. While it is indeed impossible as things stand for one person to have a pain in the body of another, there is nothing about the concepts involved that would make it absurd or impossible for us to extend or enrich our concepts to accommodate new circumstances. Compare Wittgenstein's point when he says " 'A new-born child has no teeth'—'A goose has no teeth,'—'A rose has no teeth.'—This last at any rate—one would like to say—is obviously true! It is even surer than that a goose has none.—And yet it is none too clear. For where should a rose's teeth have been? The goose has none in its jaw. And neither, of course, has it any in its wings; but no one means that when he says it has no teeth.—Why, suppose one were to say: the cow chews its food, and then dungs the rose with it, so the rose has teeth in the mouth of a beast. This would not be absurd, because one has no notion in advance where to look for teeth in a rose. [Connexion with pain in someone else's body]" (PI, pp. 221-222.)

In new and unheard of circumstances the notion of numerical identity might apply to sensations, but even here there would be a difference between the case of pain and the case of physical objects. "Which of these pains is mine?" would still fail to express a question. (Unless it was the question it now expresses. Suppose you have a new and undiagnosed discomfort. While reading a medical book you find descriptions of discomforts and pains of the appropriate kind and region. Then "Which of these pains is mine?" and "Is *this* my pain?" could be used. See PI, 411) This is important because apparently supporters of the philosophical doctrine of privacy (call them Cartesians) infer that the idea of numerical identity applies to sensations in just the way it applies to physical objects or public events from the grammatical fact that two people could be thought to have the numerically same pain under the bizarre conditions pictured. At the same time the Cartesian classifies sensations such as a pain in the finger as mental events or mental objects, i.e. as rather like thoughts and some feelings on the one hand and like familiar objects (chairs and buildings) on the other. Hence he is led to think that like thoughts, it ought to be possible that two persons should have the same sensation even in the absence of new and bizarre conditions. But on his view that would create insurmountable problems of personal identity, so the way out for the Cartesian is to *insist* on the truth of "Sensations are private" which is, after all, an obvious truism. This insistence is for him a metaphysical truth about the nature of the mental objects he calls sensations. They have at once some of the grammatical features of mental items like thoughts and some of the features of physical objects. It is this hybrid nature of sensations that contributes to the existence of the so-called problem of the knowledge of other minds in Cartesian philosophies.

Perhaps it will be objected that this argument takes a long way round in the attempt to explain the target expression. "After all, can't it be given a meaning by an ostensive or ostensive-like definition? 'Private feeling' like 'act of the will' represents a notion that can be explained ostensively." It seems that the philosopher who attempts to assign a sense to or use for the philosophical notion of an act of will has a dilemma on his hands: either 'act of will' is a mere verbal manoeuver or it still lacks a sense. Suppose he tries (what is tried) : An act of will is the willing of an action. Now of course I understand what that is. Raising my arm in usual circumstances is a case of that. But if that is what an act of the will is, then isn't it simply another way of saying that I raised my arm? "You mean by 'I performed an act of will to raise my arm' or by 'I willed to raise my arm' just what is meant by 'I raised my arm.' You can make this verbal move if you like but it seems pointless, *merely* a verbal manoeuver." On the other hand, if 'I raised my arm' doesn't capture all that is intended by 'an act of will' then the latter remains unexplained. The attempt to give it a meaning by 'pointing' to acts of the will has failed. And no amount of adding conditions will help one escape this dilemma; adding that an act of the will is raising one's arm when it's difficult to do so or when there is some likelihood of failing to do so or when trying to do so is necessary, etc. are only further verbal moves.

Parallel considerations apply to the attempt to assign a sense to the philosophical notion of private feeling or private experience. If to have a private feeling is to have a feeling that I never disclose to anyone else then of course I know what a private feeling is and what it is to have a private feeling. Typically, however, philosophers hold that private feeling *can't* be disclosed, shared, or communicated. If, in that case, the ostensive definition doesn't capture what was intended by 'private feeling,' the target expression remains without a descriptive sense.

In an interesting article[1] on the so-called private language argument, Hector-Neri Castañeda has attempted to *specify* four senses of 'private object.' Since feelings or sensations are sometimes thought of as objects, it will help to show the illegitimacy of the philosophical notion of private feeling if I bring out some of the difficulties I find in Castañeda's "definitions" of *private object*. He writes, "Now there are several senses of 'private object': (1) one which the speaker alone can (i.e. logically can) have experience of, or be acquainted with; (2) objects whose existence is (logically) determinable by the speaker alone . . . (3) objects whose possession of some characteristic A is (logically) determinable by the speaker alone. . . . (4) objects about which the speaker alone can determine for any first-order statement whether it is true or false of them . . ." (pp. 9-91) The first thing to be said about this is that if the question is: What sense can we attach to 'private' in 'private feeling'? then (1-4) must be regarded as begging this question. For the suggestion is that 'private' in 'private feeling' means what it means in 'private object' as specified in (1-4), but 'experience' 'acquainted with,' and 'determinable by the speaker,' etc. occur in (1-4) and each is sufficiently like 'feeling' and 'experience' in the original question to disqualify (1-4) on the grounds

[1] "The Private-Language Argument," in C. D. Rollins (ed.) *Knowledge and Experience* (Pittsburgh, 1963).

of circularity. It isn't a help in answering the question to be told that 'private' in 'private feeling' means what it means in 'private object,' when the latter is specified in terms such as "something of which one person alone can have experience, be acquainted with, etc."

Secondly, it isn't clear that (1-4) escape the kind of dilemma faced by the doctrine of 'acts of will.' The argument is: to assign a sense to 'private experience' by saying that it is to attach to what 'I' alone experience, etc. can be done. If to have a private experience is to have an experience that I have and no one else has, then we have a sense for 'private experience.' But this is now a pointless verbal manoeuver. If on the other hand, this isn't what is meant by 'private experience' then we haven't progressed at all.

It seems to me that the latter horn of the dilemma catches up Castañeda's moves. For except in a trivial sense, any experience I have had, someone else could have had. The feeling I had when first gazing into Grand Canyon was one I have every reason to believe many others have had before me. In this sense of "have the same feeling," there is reason to think many have had the same feeling. If it is insisted that "have the same feeling" means "have the numerically identical feeling," then as things stand the question becomes trivial and its answer with it. To deny on principle therefore that in a nontrivial sense anyone could have had the same feeling I had when first gazing into Grand Canyon is to beg the question in favor of a sense of 'private feeling' other than that of "experience never disclosed to another."

There is further evidence that Castañeda's account faces the present dilemma. He writes, "One knows . . . of his own pains by merely having them. That is, one knows of them privately." (p. 93) It is surely true that one knows of his own pains by merely having them; if this is what we are to understand by 'private feeling,' Castañeda's account is thrown back upon the other horn of the dilemma, viz., it consists in a merely verbal move.

Castañeda's first definition was that a private object is "one which the speaker alone can (i.e. logically can) have experience of, or be acquainted with." What is it that Jones alone "can (i.e. logically can) have experience of?" I take it that the answer will be on the order of "Jones' aches and pains," though not Jones' aches and pains in the sense we get in answer to questions like: What are Jones' aches and pains? For "toothache and neuritis" answers that question, and Smith can have toothache and neuritis. Philosophers want here a reference to Jones' aches and pains in answer to a question like: Which aches and pains are Jones'? where that is thought of by analogy with a question like: Which of these books and these shoes are Jones'? The analogy is faulty, however. While books and shoes can be identified in logical independence of any person, someone's aches and pains cannot. "Which aches and pains are Jones'?" has a superficial similarity to "Which books and shoes are Jones'?" But since, trivially, someone's aches and pains must be identified by reference to someone, Jones or someone else, the present question either will not arise at all, in case they are identified by reference to someone other than Jones, or it will express a logically peculiar wonder indeed, in case they are identified as Jones'. In the latter case the question turns out to express a wonder about a tautology, viz., Jones' aches and pains are Jones' aches and pains, and surely we can wonder whether "Are Jones' aches and pains Jones'?" expresses a significant question. But if not, what is it that Jones alone can (i.e. logically can) have experience of?

Consider Castañeda's second definition. A private object is an "object whose existence is (logically) determinable by the speaker alone . . ." What is an example of an "Object whose existence is (logically) determinable by the speaker alone?" His toothache? Surely we can agree that this is false, if "existence of a toothache" means "has a toothache." We often are able to determine that someone has a toothache. Furthermore, if certain of the candidates for objects that fit the second account of 'private object' are really private objects, we get the consequence that something of the type can be a private object in this sense on one occasion though not on another. For instance, suppose after-images are candidates for private objects in this sense. It seems that I can determine the existence of such an "object" in a child after popping a flash bulb in his face and getting his response. In such a case he is not the sole person capable of determining the existence of a thing. I may even have to teach him what he is experiencing. Suppose on the other hand that someone is all alone (on a desert island as philosophers say) and a strong light flashes suddenly in his eyes. It is not logically possible for anyone save the person himself to "determine the existence" of an after-image, since it is not logically possible for someone to observe him if no one is there. (I am appealing here to a logical truth such as: It is logically impossible for someone to determine the existence at a place, P, of an X the duration of which is t to t^2, when t^2 is later than t, if X leaves no trace at all after t^2 and if no one is at P during the interval t to t^2. More simply put, it is logically true that no one not in a position to experience something can experience it.) Therefore, the very same type of thing, after-image, qualifies by the second definition as a private object at one time though not at another.

(3) and (4) seem to 'define' a sense of 'private characteristic' and 'private truth' respectively rather than a sense of 'private object.' Furthermore, the considerations of the last paragraph imply that (3) qualifies what someone sees under certain conditions as a 'private object' where 'sees' is used in

such a way that "*J* sees *X*" entails that there is an *X*. For instance, suppose someone, all alone in the forest, sees a puff of smoke from an abandoned camp fire (in the present sense of 'sees'), and the puff of smoke momentarily looks to him like an opened umbrella suspended in mid-air. The puff of smoke qualifies as a private object in Castañeda's sense (3) because it has a characteristic, the look of an opened umbrella suspended in mid-air, and logically no one besides the observer can determine that it has this characteristic (by the considerations of the last paragraph). In case someone else is said to determine that it possessed this characteristic by being told that it did by the observer, we may imagine that the observer, after actually determining the characteristic in question, drops dead before telling anyone or recording what he saw. Parallel considerations hold for Castañeda's (4). If I have interpreted Castañeda's (1-4) correctly, they fail to specify a sense of 'private object' in the philosophically interesting and required way. For things other than things like pains and after-images qualify, and pains and after-images don't always qualify.

Almost everything I have said so far has been negative. In what follows I shall attempt to clarify a positive view of the association between 'private' and 'feeling.'

First of all, we learn to keep things secret; we have to acquire the ability of suppressing our feelings. Part of what is involved in learning to replace natural and instinctive expressions of feeling by conventional and linguistic expressions of them is the ability to *keep from* employing conventional expressions when one wants. Indeed, it seems to be part of the point of such conventional practices that they need not always be invoked by someone suffering an ache or pain or fear or remorse. Part of mastering these conventions is, therefore, acquiring the ability to fit the convention to the occasion. The occasion may include both the fact that one is suffering some ache or pain and one's other circumstances at the time. For official and solemn occasions we have learned to keep our feelings to ourselves; if we haven't, we are left open to the censure imposed on violations of such conventions as there are for such occasions.

Secondly, it follows that keeping feelings private and secret is a "derivative" or "secondary" ability, and an ability or skill which requires the exercise of care and will. For it would hardly be reasonable to impose such censure upon emotional outbursts in public places as we sometimes do or even to have the means in our language to do so if expressing our feelings were the unnatural, difficult, and problematic activity it is in principle pictured to be by some philosophers. When we fail in expression it is normally a failure to keep quiet, secret, and private rather than a failure to publicize. And this may be due to a failure of will or a failure to take care in ordering one's surroundings to fit one's will. Furthermore, keeping something to oneself, keeping it private, and keeping it a secret are things we learn how to do only after we have learned how to express the matter in question. For keeping it private precisely is an *abstention*. One cannot abstain from nothing in particular; abstinence takes an object. So abstaining from telling all, from expressing one's feelings, presupposes that one could tell all and could express one's feelings if it were desirable to do so. In this sense, being able to express one's feelings in the usual conventional ways is a "primary" ability, and being able to abstain from such expression is a "secondary" ability.

Two of the elements of the positive view I am attempting to clarify are, therefore: (1) Keeping one's feelings private in the sense of keeping them to oneself is something one learns to do; it is not part of the "natural predicament of man," the so-called "egocentric predicament," etc. (2) It is an ability that presupposes the ability to express one's feel-

ings by means of the usual conventional and linguistic de-
vices of our language. A third element is implicit in this picture. It is the familiar but notoriously difficult notion that
(3), there is a "not merely contingent" relation between
feeling and expression. This feature is inherited by the relation of the substituted conventional expressions of feelings
and feelings. By a non-contingent relation I mean what is
sometimes referred to as a "logical" connection or a conceptual connection. Thus, to have a certain feeling or a feeling of a certain sort is to engage in expressing or be disposed
to engage in expressing oneself in a certain way; by means
of pain behaviour in case of pain, by aggression behaviour
in case of anger, and by means of praise and adoration in
the case of religious emotions, etc. (3) does not entail that it
is impossible to have a feeling but not express it; (3) does
entail that it makes no sense to say that there is a feeling of
which there is no such thing as its expression (unless it is
an inexpressible feeling. But in context that phrase expresses
a feeling). (3) does not require that "expression" is taken
in "a behaviouristic sense," whatever that may be. Different
and extraordinarily complicated forms of action express the
subtler emotions; the forms of simulation of such feelings
are virtually as complex. The more ways there are for expressing emotions, the more ways there are for dissembling,
disguising, feigning, concealing, and keeping private one's
true feeling. (Perhaps also the more ways there are for expressing an emotion, the more there is to express.)

I know of no conclusive arguments in support of (1), (2)
and (3). (1) seems to me to be a fact about people, viz., they
aren't naturally secretive. Children must be taught to keep
things to themselves—their aches and pains, the family
scandals, and their feelings about adults.

(2) is the thesis that a person cannot be said to keep from
expressing himself (his feelings, emotion, aches and pains)

unless he knows how to express himself, and to know how to express one's feelings (in other ways than by natural, instinctive movement) is to have acquired in some degree the linguistic means for doing so. These in turn are a consequence of the social conventions and institutions of our life. An argument in support of (2) rests on the logical points that (i) "Keeping from expressing" requires an object, that is, something that one keeps from expressing, and (ii) "Keeping from expressing" itself expresses an action or something for which one can be blamed, an act of omission. Hence, if there is nothing that a person is able to express because he lacks the techniques or language for its expression, then there is nothing that he can refrain from expressing; keeping one's feelings private presupposes the ability to express them and hence it presupposes a mastery of the linguistic and other techniques for such expression. And since being secretive or keeping one's feelings private is something one does (an omission or abstention), this piece of action itself has typical forms which need to be mastered in order to succeed in such acts. In short, one can't keep anything to himself unless he first has it, has a way of expressing it, and has some of the technique for keeping it to himself.

As for arguments in support of (3), the shortest is that (1) and (2) are true and presuppose (3). Consider also that some feelings in some circumstances ought to be kept private; others, in some circumstances, ought not to be kept private. We reserve such epithets as 'insincere,' 'disingenuous,' and even 'hypocritical' for people who keep their true feelings a secret in those circumstances in which they oughtn't to. A bore is censured for not keeping things private, but the quality of our censure of a hypocrite is harsher than that of a mere bore. This wouldn't make sense unless there was an intimate association between having a certain feeling and being disposed to act in a certain way. This association or connection is described in (3) as a conceptual or logical connection.

In conclusion, therefore, the association between 'private' and 'feeling' is no closer than that between 'private' and anything else. But it is of more interest in the case of feelings, since it is true that we *can* keep our feelings to ourselves, and we are sometimes open to censure for not doing so. I take the fact of this special interest as further confirmation of the view of private feeling expressed above.[2]

[2] This is a somewhat expanded version of the essay which appeared in *The Southern Journal of Philosophy*. I thank the editor for permission to include some revisions.

IV

The Sense of the Senses

by Erwin W. Straus

In a book entitled *The Neurophysiological Basis of Mind,* John C. Eccles published in 1953 his Wayneflete Lectures. There the author, now Sir John Eccles, presented in a systematic order the results of his studies on synaptic transmis-

Erwin W. Straus was educated at the Universities of Munich, Zurich, Goettingen, and Berlin (M.D., 1919). In addition to his work as a psychiatrist, he has taught at the University of Berlin, Black Mountain College (North Carolina), University of Kentucky (as lecturer), at the Universities of Frankfurt, Würzburg, Duquesne, and the University of California at Santa Cruz. Formerly Director of Professional Education and Research at the Veterans Administration Hospital at Lexington, Kentucky, he is currently Research Consultant there as well as Clinical Professor of Psychiatry at the University of Kentucky. His honors—too numerous to list—include the degrees of Doctor of Philosophy (h.c.) from the University of Würzburg and Doctor of Laws (h.c.) from the University of Kentucky. Among his many books are *Wesen und Vorgang der Suggestion, Geschehnis und Erlebnis, Vom Sinn der Sinne* (2nd ed.; tr. as *The Primary World of the Senses*), *Psychologie der Menschlichen Welt, Phenomenological Psychology: Selected Papers,* and *On Obsession.*

sion, a piece of successful research honored with a Nobel Prize. It seems, therefore, justified to take this book as a model representative for the scientist's approach to the mind-body problem, or rather to the body-mind problem; for, notwithstanding the fact that Eccles registers as a dualist, he does not start from the *cogito*. Convinced that Science— thanks to the enriched inventory of neurophysiological methods and techniques—at long last offers a solution for that age-old problem, Eccles presents in the first seven chapters of his book the principles of neurophysiology, as forecast by the subtitle. At the end, when it finally seems well established how the brain works as a machine, the author resumes in the 25 pages of the last chapter the question where, when, and how a "liaison between mind and brain could occur." (Preface, VI). One quickly realizes that not much action space can be left to the mind when it sneaks into that attic already crowded with all those circuits reverberating and with those countless electric impulses arriving or departing.

Although this last chapter is conceived as an extension of the Principles of Neurophysiology, a radical change of atmosphere occurs as soon as the "ghost enters into the machine." [1] The brain explored by the neurophysiologist and the brain with which the mind enters into liaison are not the same.

In the first seven chapters the neurophysiologist, reporting his observations, speaks as one who shares the world of visible, audible, tangible things with other living creatures, a world in which he is free to move from his home to his laboratory and from Canberra, Australia, to Oxford, England. In his lectures Eccles addressed his audience as his partners who found themselves together with him in the world (Lebenswelt), not peeping through a mysterious peri-

---

[1] Cp. Ryle, G. *The Concept of Mind.* Hutchinson's University Library, London, 1949.

scope into an external establishment. As long as Eccles describes nerves and brains he refers to them as parts of his own environment, but when he invites the mind to enter into liaison with the brain, the brain undergoes a sudden metamorphosis. Now the brain is no longer a part of the observer's world; instead, as Russell Brain wrote, ". . . the perceptual world . . . the whole realm of our perceptual experience, is a construct of the percipient's brain." [2] Thus the percipient's brain, floating in space, passes through indeterminable whereabouts. The mind is the luckless master of that habitat, a Noah who forgot to bring wife and sons and living creatures, two of every sort, into the Ark. All alone by himself he is unable to send even a dove on a test flight, because there are no birds and his Ark has no window. The mind, cut off from the world and from communication, starts its work as a captive, confined to play with the tinsel of sensa and percepts. How these phantoms enter and how they are projected outward remains a secret.

Eccles' book is apparently divided into a large scientific and a small philosophical section where the author does his best to secure a tiny area of autonomy for the mind. Actually the book is based from its very beginning on a hidden metaphysical dogma, one could rightly say *the* metaphysical dogma accepted by the great majority of scientists. The credo is that the brain belongs to the realm of genuine reality while "mental" experience merely accompanies, or perhaps on occasion interferes with, the real events.[3] It seems, therefore, fully justified to turn the attention first to the working machine—the brain—and to reduce and adapt experience to the

[2] Brain, Sir Russell. *The Nature of Experience.* Oxford University Press, 1959, p. 24.

[3] Eccles presents the hypothesis that "only when there is a high level of activity in the cortex (as revealed by the electro-encephalogram) is liaison with mind possible." (p. 265).

functions of the underlying structure. Yet, following this line of orthodox interpretation, we find ourselves entangled in unexpected difficulties, since we cannot ignore that two brains are involved in neurophysiological research: the brain observed and the observer's brain. All principal tenets must be valid for the observer's brain in the first place; for the observer, not the observed, is responsible for an observation. Experimental cats and dogs, rats and monkeys don't talk; the brains handled by the anatomist, the pathologist, the neurosurgeon, are not a bit more communicative. It is the observer who arranges, who opens and ends, describes and reports, an experiment—whatever its topic may be. Since, however, the dogma postulates that all mental activities can and must be reduced to cerebral functions, the observer's brain is finally enthroned as the real agent.[4] The alleged ontological principle requires that an observation occurs in the machine of the observer's brain, and must therefore be considered as an event confined to one particular place and time. Certainly, the observer's brain does not know of any other brain; a machine among machines, it is exposed—but also limited—to causal interference, to stimuli arriving from over there, but acting exclusively on the receptors attached to the observer's nervous system. "It becomes ever clearer," says Percival Bailey, "that the concepts that we gather under the term 'mental' are only names given to various aspects of the

---

[4] Actually, the roles of the two brains are not exchangeable. The observer's brain is not an object of observation—certainly not for the observer himself. Yet in an inquiry concerned with the problem how "the brain achieves liaison with the mind" (Eccles, p. 260) there is a trend to substitute the brain observed for the observer's brain. The very phenomena of perceiving, observing, thinking, the relation of man as observer to things observable and observed are bypassed. Compare "Man Thinks, Not the Brain" in my monograph, *The Primary World of Senses* (Part III), The Free Press of Glencoe, New York, 1963.

functioning of the cerebral cortex." [5] Measured then by his own standards, we must consider the writer's statements as mere output from his nervous system. "Thought is a name we give to the functioning of our thinking machine (cortex), just as flight is a name we give to the functioning of flying machines." (p. 7) If the information given by the author is nothing but an echo of events in his own cortex, are we not forced to conclude that the individual cortex must actually know itself? If this were so, we should wonder that—instead of mere intuition—the full exertion of neurophysiological research is required and how it is possible. Furthermore, how can we account for the fact that the knowledgeable cortex needs, in spite of its own microstructure, instruments of magnification in the exploration of other brains?

Unaware that he condemned himself to the role of a cerebroloquist or corticoloquist, Bailey talked on two different levels. On the upper level he addressed an audience as the keynote speaker; on the lower level Bailey's brain (cortex) handled signals or functions "like a missile guided to its goal by a thermionic machine." (pp. 4 and 10). On the upper level the speaker used the pronoun "we": "The word 'mind' is a verbal symbol that we use to refer to the activity of the cerebral cortex." (p. 10). On the lower level the cortex functions as an isolated aggregate: brains do not enter into a "we" group. Listening to a speaker, we in the audience understand him not as a signaling brain but as a person, an experiencing human being through whose mouth we may gain information about events or conditions unknown to us, as, for instance, about the true functions of the brain cortex. From Bailey's point of view the cortex appears in three different roles: (a) as a speaker's cortex (releasing and han-

[5] Bailey, P. "Cortex and Mind" in *Theories of the Mind,* Chapter 1, Edited by J. Sheer, Free Press of Glencoe, New York, 1962, p. 8.

dling symbols); (b) as a listener's cortex (receiving signals) and (c) as the brain and cortex (the topic, selected for the speaker's address). How a listener's cortex, stimulated through a speaker's cortex, could ever establish a relation to the cortex No. 3 is a scientific *mysterium*.

At the end of his paper Bailey congratulated himself on his solution of the mind-cortex problem; solved "to his own satisfaction, if to no one else's," he added (p. 12). Bailey was satisfied, although he had not checked the strength of his doctrine with the crucial test of applying it to himself. His diction is boastful, to be sure; yet his attitude is not a passing expression at the moment of a personal triumph; it is quite typical for those who try to explore the neurophysiological basis of mind. Most of them, if not all, ignore the presence of the two brains and therefore fail to realize their different roles in observation. They do not reflect upon themselves. Instead, they turn their attention exclusively to the brain observed as object of their studies. They explore the brain as a quasi independent aggregate, joined with an animal's body like an automobile motor is attached to the body of a car. Once the essential features of the behavior of the nervous system are known an attempt is made to relate or to reduce the 'facts of experience' to that "cerebral 'machine' operating according to the laws of physics and chemistry." That whole area of research is considered as a dominion of Science, which is never questioned in this hysteron proteron about its place in the human world, nor about its origin in human perception and thought. Like Athena, who according to Greek mythology burst forth from Zeus' head in her full armor, Science appears on the scene with all her equipment and techniques.

Since the reflex schema serves as model for the exploration of the cerebral functions, the essential characteristics of sensory experience, its openness, the relation of an experiencing creature to an object qua object are eliminated from the beginning.

Yet, to all this there is one exception. The observer claims a privileged status for himself. He and his brain are not submitted to the strict rules of reduction; they must be exempted; otherwise experiment and observation would come to a sudden end. In effect, the observer brings along into the laboratory the whole repertoire of attitudes familiar in the Lebenswelt.

Eccles presents the principle of neurophysiology without any epistemological scruples in the naive attitude of everyday life. When the mind-brain problem is finally brought up for discussion, the mind is treated in the third person, like a quasi physical object, a junior partner of the brain. Eccles seems not to notice that from the beginning "the mind" looks over his shoulders, directs his sight, and guides his hands. Eccles lectures. Yet language, speech, communication, the transformation of the spoken into the written and printed words—all these accomplishments are not raised even to the rank of problems, as should be done by one who wants to establish the neurophysiological basis of mind. His book contains—as one may expect—many illustrations, diagrams, curves, schemata, but once again the possibility of pictorial representation is not discussed; neither are experimentation, the raising of questions, the consideration of possibilities, the experimental answers and decisions honored as mental performances. Just as we are accustomed to find and to use forks and knives at a dinner table, so Eccles applies scientific methods to the exploration of the nervous system. He simply takes them for granted. Unimpressed by the fact that all of them are human inventions, he is not concerned to investigate what enables man to function as *homo sapiens* or *homo faber*. Eccles presents hypotheses; he mentions predictions and their verification—apparently unaware that he had already entered the mind's workshop. But instead of extending this list any further we may point out some mental contributions implied in the application of one particular method: the EEG.

A physician, a biologist, who interprets an EEG has to be familiar with the typical variations of the records; he has to be informed about the alpha and all the other Greek letter rhythms; he must be cognizant of the low-medium-high-voltage waves and their significance; in short, he has to know a great number of details established through world-wide research during the 35 years following Berger's discovery. All such details the expert has to learn. Yet the application of his specific knowledge demands a much wider, unspecific but indispensable, comprehension. This wisdom—not taught in any school— may be taken for granted in the practice of everyday life. But those who search for the neurophysiological basis of mind must waive that privilege of artlessness. It is their task to discover the problems hidden in the obvious.

(1) A completed EEG record is a rather simple device, consisting of a long strip of paper with groups of 4, 6, or 8 curved lines inscribed. The paper—the ground—and the lines—the figure—are seen simultaneously. Yet the correct interpretation of an EEG demands that we do not accept this figure-ground relation as it appears at the time of inspection. Contrary to the physiological conditions which present figure and ground simultaneously, we must understand the EEG chart like a kind of historical document. We must realize that the curved lines have been added at some time in the past to the blank paper. The analysis of details requires a reconstruction of their origin, a regression—in thoughts—directed against the current of time, from the present to the past. This procedure of reconstructing is not an act of remembering. The acta embodied in the EEG do not belong to the interpreter's personal past. Those events occurred in

the objective temporal order of things; but the blank relation earlier-later will not do either. We are concerned with things in a state of becoming; the once untouched paper underwent a permanent change. We see it after the transformation has occurred; but we understand those black curves as the lasting effect of the transitory action of the fingers of the EEG machine; we recapture in our thoughts that past process in *statu nascendi.* In our interpretation of the EEG we move against the original current of time, from the effect to the cause—as we do in most, if not all, cases in search for causal determination.

Our interpretation is not determined by "stimuli." They act in the very moment of inspection only, following each other in the sequence of a fast pulsating clock; they may produce an aftereffect, but they have no history.[6] The stimuli did not undergo a change; the chart did. Our interpretation therefore transcends the present stimulus situation; it is concerned with the EEG as a visible object. It silently acknowledges the fundamental difference between optical stimuli and visible things, between our acts of seeing and the organization of things seen. The interpretation of an EEG requires a temporal horizon within which earlier and later, past and present, events are accessible to one comprehensive view. The interpretation which occurs at a specific moment in time demands an understanding of time, transcending the actual moment.

In relating the permanent writ to the transitory writing of the machine we have reached only the first base, or rather the last one, since the direction of our home run is inverted. We must also realize that the movements of the hands were in turn determined by the once present electro-potential dif-

---

[6] Recourse to the so-called reverberating circuits does not help, because the circuitous reverberations would function only as actual events in rapid succession.

ferences in the various brain regions of a patient. Confront-
ed, e.g., with bilaterally synchronous spike waves, we may
suspect that such irregularity might have been caused by an
anomalous function of the temporal lobes. Continuing our
retracing into the past, we may wonder whether this mal-
function may not have provoked a psychomotor attack in a
still earlier period. Then, with a sudden jump from the past
to the present, an expert giving his opinion in court may
suggest that the defendant of today was not responsible for
the indicted action, committed in the past.

While the machinery of the brain functioning in accor-
dance with the laws of physics and chemistry operates in
the one-way direction of physical time, we move freely from
the present to the past and from the past to the present.

(2). Having completed the interpretation of an EEG in
terms of the chronicler's time, we are ready for the next step.
We may now turn our attention to the frozen lines themselves. On the chart nothing moves; the curves are perfectly
at rest, comparable to the contours of a woodcut; however,
since we know that those lines presently seen at rest had
been produced by the writing fingers of the machine, we consider these precipitates as residues of action. We bring them
in our minds back into motion; we speak about rhythms,
counting the number of beats (or spikes) per second. We
look at the chart as if those lines were still completing their
itinerary; we add a horizontal line which we claim represents
time and temporal extension. Yet the represented order is by
two steps remote from actual experience: first there is the
contrast between the rest actually seen and the biased interpretation of motion, and, second, there is a striking difference between the actual experience of time and its representation on the chart. In our experience beginning and end
of a second, or a minute, do not coincide. Nevertheless, on the
chart we do see the beginning and the end of one or two, or

ten seconds, simultaneously. The possibility of comprehending beginning and end of a second at one glance permits us to count the number of oscillations per temporal unit and to speak of rhythms, just as if these curves actually moved up and down.

I do not intend to criticize this procedure as such; I do not bewail that lived-time has been replaced by time extended in space. I only want to point out: (1) how complex those apparently simple and familiar procedures are; (2) that the "mind" must have been active in the conception and execution of these techniques; and (3) that it is at least doubtful whether one could ascribe such accomplishments to the brain, considered as a machine.

(3). Because EEG records are of considerable length, the individual chart, folded in accordion pleats, is handled like a book; the curves are read from left to right, the leaves turned from right to left. Between turns only a segment of the whole record is visible. Whenever necessary the interpreter of an EEG will reverse the directions and return after the study of a later to an earlier section, moving from the end toward the beginning. There is nothing remarkable in this procedure; the situation, however, is radically changed the very moment we try to account for it in strictly physiological terms.

(a). While we understand that the visible segments are extended and continued beyond the border of the page just read, the bundles of optical stimuli reflected from each page do not form a continuum. Confined to the actual moment, they are not open to the future, to what is not yet. If it is true that single data fixed to particular moments on the axis of physical time are the original givens, this situation cannot be corrected through experience or learning.

(b). To turn a page is no demanding assignment. Unfortunately, the news of the accomplished task never reaches the optical cortex. The area calcarina has no direct relation to a visible object as such. The connection is mediated through light, a physical agent transformed into an optical stimulus the moment it hits the retina. Whether the light is reflected from the front or from the back of a page makes no difference; in both cases light travels in the same direction. Stimuli are not turned when we turn a page. The direction cornea-retina-calcarina remains invariant throughout our lives. The "information" dispatched from the retina over the optical pathways enters the area striata always through the same door. All the afferent impulses move over a one-way street. Whether, and how, the cortex could organize the "real" sequence of two uni-directional excitations into the apparent relation of front and back is at best an open question.

(c). While we reverse the sequence, turn the pages back from end to beginning, in our action we move on with clock time—with the cerebral pulse, if you want. Such performance is but one variation of the theme of re-peating, re-hearsing, re-capitulating. Let us suppose we compare on the record a period during which the patient kept his eyes open with the *preceding* one, taken while he had his eyes closed, then our inspection of the earlier part actually follows that of the later one. There we encounter once again the contrast between the temporal order of our act of seeing and the order of things seen.

(d). In turning a page from obverse to reverse I direct my attention to an object there in front of me, a substantial thing visible to me and to others in my neighborhood. We do not gaze into an external world; we and the chart belong to the same terrestrial area. While I see the chart I also see my own hand on the same plane. I touch and grasp the visible leaf with my fingers, and in turning my forearm and hand I also turn the page.

The physiological interpretation of this situation strictly contradicts direct experience in most aspects. The intentional relation to the object has been completely eliminated. Instead, the investigator's interest is centered on heterogeneous stimuli, which acting upon diverse exteroceptive and proprioceptive receptors release in an isolated organism centripetal impulses transmitted over widely distant pathways to separate cortical areas. These regions, whatever their fiber communications are, do not communicate with each other. Should there be a simultaneity of excitations, it must go unnoticed, since none of the areas are aware of time. In any case, temporal coincidence could not represent sensory correlation and integration. In turning a page we do not add tactile to optical impressions; we touch the colorful, visible things; we do not touch colors. The same object is accessible to us in various modalities, although sight and touch do not provide identical information; I cannot read an EEG curve with my fingers. Yet I can point to and mark with my finger tip one spot on the visible page, although retinal cones and Meissner's corpuscles are located far apart from each other in my body. The physiological account leads into an impasse. The way back to everyday life is blocked. The original object of action—the page to be turned—disappeared completely from the scene.

4. An EEG record is a "public" document. Taken by a technician, sent to a ward through hospital mail, it will finally be read by a physician who in turn may demonstrate his findings to a resident. Nobody who plays a role in this little drama ever stops to wonder that and how this transaction is possible. Indeed, in the practice of everyday life communication with the "alter ego" is taken for granted. Since Methusela's days trade has been based on the never disputed or questioned conviction that in buying and selling, in giving and taking, goods change hands. The technician who

placed the EEG record into the mail, the messenger who carried it, the secretary who received it, the doctor who read it—all of them had not the slightest doubt that the same material thing had passed from hand to hand. The mail carrier would be highly surprised if he were asked whether he brought the technician's stimuli along with him. An expert who teaches a student to read an EEG also takes it for granted that both of them see the same object together, notwithstanding the fact that two bodies, two separate nervous systems, affected by two different sets of stimuli are involved. Persisting in the everyday life attitude, the expert solves the startling problems concerning intersubjectivity, the alter ego, the possibility of communication, by the simple method of ignoring them. How to prepare scrambled eggs, how to use a typewriter, such skills we must learn. Into the mysteries of communication we are initiated without any effort on our part by nature itself. "We" includes children and animals. The moment, however, we leave the market place and enter the philosopher's studio our naive confidence is shaken. We are asked to vote either for inference or empathy, for appresentation or Being-with. Science which demands that data must be public is finally forced to reject its own postulate. For brains do not communicate; stimuli are strictly private; the light rays which pass through Jones' pupils will never reach Miller's retina. Yet the members of the audience in the theater, the spectators in a stadium, see altogether the same play or watch the same game. True, each one sees for himself, each one from his own particular position, in an always limited perspective. Nevertheless all of them witness the same show. The view is one; the viewers are many. The view is public; the sights are private.

Sensory experience opens the world to us. Objects become accessible qua objects. ". . . the thing known, or the thing of which a subject is aware, must, despite its being other and elsewhere than the subject, nevertheless be present to the knowing subject." [7] Sensory experience is neither a mere reception of hyletic data nor a pure act of spontaneity. In touching something we are in contact, touched ourselves. To see the wonders of the world we must travel, go where they are; they present themselves to us, when we expose ourselves to them, when we—as one says—cast an eye upon them. We see them at a distance, but we do not place them in an outside world. We see them over there from our own position here in mundane space. In sensory experience we are aware of things and of ourselves in our bodily existence. This relation has no counterpart in the realm of inanimate things. [8]

Day after day millions of people all over the globe attend the movie theaters. To see and to enjoy a film as such requires no special training; no effort is involved; nobody in a typical audience lays claim to an unusual accomplishment. The millions of movie-goers demonstrate—as through a gigantic experiment—that the capacity to see such pictures must be a character inherent in visual experience. Effortless in practice, it nevertheless strikes us with wonder.

Calling the film a moving *picture,* we silently acknowledge that the actors seen were not present in person, that the stage on which they worked was not a part of our environment. Yet we saw the subjects and saw them with our own eyes. The *physiological* conditions that enabled us to follow their performance did in principle not differ from seeing our neighbors, the walls, the screen itself before and after the show. The subjects on the screen were acting. There was a temporal sequence, a beginnning and an end of their at-

[7] Veatch, Henry B. "Minds: What and Where are They?" In: *Theories of the Mind.*

[8] Cp. Straus, E. *The Primary World of Senses.* Free Press of Glencoe, New York, 1963, Part IV, Chapter B, "Sensing considered as a mode of communication."

tempts to deal with the plot, but the time of their action was not that of our own present.

This is of course true for every picture, be it a still picture or a movie. The photos printed in a newspaper, the events shown on a news reel represent something that has happened somewhere else at some other time in the past. Obviously, in viewing a picture or film two temporal orders are conjoined: one of our personal present and act of seeing, the other the temporal order of things and actions seen. We witness past events as past, though in the present. From such observations we conclude that sensory experience has a polar structure: it comprises my own act of seeing and the things seen.

Physiology, bound by philosophical tradition, interprets sensory experience as a process of incorporation, comparable to eating and breathing. In principle there is no difference between the effects of light, provoking pigmentation of skin, or releasing a contraction of the pupils or stimulating the optical cortex. To restore some kinship with everyday life experience physiology therefore was forced to take refuge in the flimsy hypothesis of an outward projection, which, however, in spite of its paramount importance, is treated in a cavalier manner. In textbooks and monographs a few lines must do. Maybe this is actually not so surprising; not much is said— because not much can be said. There is no observation, let alone demonstration or measurement, which could support the hypothesis. After all, who performs the projection? The mind? the soul? the brain?. The mind, says Eccles; the brain, says Russell Brain. Actually the two authors are not too far apart from each other. If it were the brain, what does it project? Cells? DNA? electropotentials? sensa? If the sensa, on what screen? Into what segment of space are they projected? Where are they located after the projection? Perhaps in the external world? Yet if you throw something out the window, this something is gone; it will no longer be inside your room. Or must we assume that the projected sensa are somehow held back like a kite? Obviously the term projection must not be used literally as if it was signifying a maneuver of cerebral transportation. Yet if we accept "externalization" as a kind of metaphor, a reference to, a representation of, sensory data based on cues, judgments, we tumble from Scylla into Charybdis. How is it that my projected sensa could become visible to someone else who, after all, must also be a character of my own projection?

According to Russell Brain, "the perceptual world . . . the whole realm of our perceptual experience, is a construct of the percipient's brain." [9] Yet, if "colors, sounds, smells, and touches are generated by the brain of the percipient," [10] then, obviously, the percipient and his brain both are constructs of Lord Brain's brain, and so on ad infinitum. In medical parlance the word "brain" signifies an organ that, when laid open to inspection, becomes visible in its size, shape, and colors, a thing of a certain weight and density, smell and temperature—in short, it appears endowed with all those "qualitative features" that have "no resemblance to the physical object which it represents." [11] The generating brain which constructs the perceptual world cannot be identical with the constructed one. Yet it is this brain, with its hemispheres and lobes, fissures and gyri, with its gray and white matter, where a neurologist may locate a tumor and invite a surgeon to remove it. How is it possible that the several brains of all those attending the operation converge in one common view although each is stimulated by a particular group of "external events"? Furthermore, does the surgeon operate on his own externalized sensa, or does he cut into a

[9] Cp. this paper, above.
[10] R. Brain, page 10.
[11] R. Brain, page 24.

human body? Does man, insofar as he in his corporeal existence sees, hears, smells himself, generate his own image?
How can the generating brain ever recognize its own condition and analyze it critically, in spite of its innate and in-
curable propensity to produce sensory percepts? Why does
the mirage of the perceptual world persist once its illusory
character has been discovered? Is science not also a human
construct? Is the mathematical world not also related to the
human brain?

While Eccles had planned to present the neurophysiological basis of mind, the mind actually had been at work
throughout, directing observation and description from the
beginning. Since the presence of this stowaway went unnoticed, it is not surprising that the part finally assigned to
the ghost in the machine is pitifully meager.

Through its liaison with an individual brain the mind is
necessarily confined to a private world. The escape designed
by Eccles is impassible; the emergency door cannot be
opened from inside. The mind operates in willed action in
the brain, where "some specific spatial-temporal pattern of
neuronal activity in the cerebral cortex evoke a percept in
the mind." [12] Those percepts then "are projected somewhere
outside the cortex." [13] If that mind happens to be a scientist's mind, it has "to build up a progressively more valid or
real physical world," a world "more and more purified from
the symbolic bias" of colors, sounds, smells, etc. The perceptual world need not be purified had it not been polluted in
the first place. Following his spiritual ancestors in a great
distance, Eccles uses the word "purified" without any moral
or religious implications. He simply expects the scientists
to purge themselves from any contamination with secondary
qualities; and who would not prefer the valid to the un-

[12] p. 263.
[13] p. 263.

valid, the real to the unreal? Even so, one may wonder whether anybody given a chance would ever make his home in the purified zone. In all probability they would prefer to stay with the rest of us in that familiar region which carries the stigma of unreality, where colors and sounds prevail even when brandished as confused ideas and denounced as fancies and apparitions, "merely symbolic of events in the physical world with which they are quite unlike." [14] Nobody would volunteer for the fate of Helen Keller.

Eddington's famous parable of his two tables may help us to illuminate the situation, even beyond its author's own intention.

"I have settled down to the task of writing these lectures," he begins the Introduction to *The Nature of the Physical World*, "and have drawn up my chairs to my two tables. Two tables! Yes, there are duplicates of every object about me—two tables, two chairs, two pens. . . . One of them has been familiar to me from earliest years. It is a commonplace object of that environment which I call the world. . . . It has extension; it is comparatively permanent; it is colored; above all it is *substantial*. . . . Table No. 2 is my scientific table. . . . My scientific table is mostly emptiness. Sparsely scattered in that emptiness are numerous electric charges rushing about with great speed; but their combined bulk amounts to less than a billionth of the bulk of the table itself. Notwithstanding . . . it supports my writing paper as satisfactorily as table number one; for when I lay the paper on it the little electric particles with their headlong speed keep on hitting the under side, so the paper is maintained in shuttlecock fashion about my second table."

Eddington is convinced that his "second scientific table" is the "only one which is really there—wherever 'there' may

[14] Eccles, page 280.

be"; but he is no less sure "that modern physics will never succeed in exorcising that first table." This ambivalence is due to one characteristic defect of his fascinating story. Like so many others, he fails to apply his methods to himself. He speaks of every object about him but overlooks that in line with the two tables, two chairs, two pens, there must also be two Eddingtons.

Eddington did not descend in person into the world of shadows. Comfortably seated at his familiar table he lifted the lid from the world below and thereby discovered that his aboding was a "strange compound of external nature, mental imagery and inherited prejudice." "In removing our illusions," Eddington stated, "we have removed the substance, for indeed, we have seen that substance is one of the greatest of our illusions." His discovery of illusions, however, remained without effect; it did not change his lived reality. Eddington discovered the illusions, but did not wonder how any illusion could have come into being, if the physicist's world is the "only one which is really there." Obviously there could be no illusions in that primary world—but no insight, no physics either. The world of shadows does not know itself. There is no ascent possible from the lower to the upper level.

Eddington places pointer-reading high on the list of scientific techniques. Yet, pointers don't read themselves, not even those of the self-registering type. Pointers are read exclusively in our familiar world. There the reader must be able to visualize the instrument in its stability and permanence; he must understand that the scale presents in one arrangement many possibilities; he must realize that the hand marks as actual one of the possible positions; he finally must conjoin two separate events in one personal "now".

On the level of table No. 2 pointer and reader are eliminated. Nevertheless, Eddington speaks about "my scientific table." But the usage of these attributes is not justified: a) the possessive relations mine, yours, his, and likewise the demonstrative "this", vanished with the speaking person. b). the ending "—fic" in the word scientific, related to the Latin "facere", refers to the scienti-ficer, the science-maker. A table, however, does not make science—nor is it made by science. Scientific is the given interpretation; the structure of table No. 2 is constructed by man, who as the knower, reaches beyond the known. The power, gained by men through sensory experience, science, and technique clearly indicates that man's position in nature is superior to the things dominated by him. The perceptual world needs no purification because, with our presence in our perceptual world the relation to objects qua objects is first established in an open horizon of space and time.

At this point I may venture a prediction about the future of the philosophy of mind: the case of sensory experience will be brought before a Court of Appeal with the intention to revise the verdict of its epistemological and ontological inferiority. It will be demonstrated during this trial that and how mental life is related in all its manifestations, not just to the mechanisms of the brain, but to the live body as a whole.

V

Problems in the Philosophy of Mind

by Edward H. Madden

The phrase philosophy of mind refers to an analysis of 'mental' and 'physical' and to a specification of the relationships between these concepts. It refers in fact to nothing new but to a traditional cluster of problems about perception and the mind-body relationship. No one in the past thirty years, I believe, has given a more coherent and promising analysis of this cluster of problems than Professor C. J. Ducasse. I will first briefly inquire into the nature of Ducasse's views and then proceed to show how he avoids many

Edward H. Madden was educated at Oberlin and the University of Iowa (Ph.D., 1950). He has taught at the University of Connecticut, San Jose State College, and is currently Professor of Philosophy at the State University of New York at Buffalo. He has served as visiting professor at Brown and Amherst, is general editor of the series, "Harvard Source Books in the History of Science," and has been president of the Peirce Society. He is the author of *The Structure of Scientific Thought, Philosophical Problems of Psychology, Chauncey Wright and the Foundations of Pragmatism,* and other books.

of the usual pitfalls. The overall effect of this discussion is designed to shed light on the numerous issues which have been discussed in the present series of articles on the philosophy of mind.

1.

Assume that I am concentrating on hue and experience a completely specific blue ("completely specific" being here the equivalent of W. E. Johnson's technical term "determinate") and express this fact by saying that "I sense this blue." Such a statement is misleadingly similar to "I see a chair" and might suggest that a sensation is somehow an object of sensing. In fact the analyses of the two sentences are quite different. The chair is the object of my perceiving and exists independently of it, while blue is not the object of my sensing and does not exist independently of it. Experiencing blue is a species or kind of sensing, and its whole *esse* consists in that sensing. Or, putting the point another way, sensing is an adverbial and not a substantive matter— "I see bluely," not "I see this blue." In the specific terminology of Ducasse, 'chair' is an adventitious or alien accusative of experiencing, while 'blue' is a connate accusative of experiencing.[1] Given these distinctions, one is able to distinguish between the concepts of physical and mental in the following way: 'physical' refers to an object of perception, the *esse* of which is not its *experiri,* while 'mental' refers to a species of experiencing whose *esse* is its *experiri,* and which is never an object of perception but is sometimes an object of *introspection,* or of *recollection,* or of a mental act of some other kind.[2]

[1] C. J. Ducasse, *Nature, Mind, and Death* (La Salle, Illinois: Open Court Publishing Company, 1951), chapter 13.

[2] Ducasse, "Minds, Matter and Bodies," in *Brain and Mind,* ed. J. R. Smythies (New York: Humanities Press, 1965).

It follows from the above that sensations are epistemically primary and perceptions are always *interpretations*. One interprets his complex of sensations as remote effects of nonpsychical occurrences of which he is never directly aware. "To perceive visually for instance an apple is to sense visually together certain colour-qualities, shapes, sizes and relations; and to interpret them as remotely caused under the existing circumstances (presence of an eye, optic nerve, etc.) by exercise of a relevant capacity (capacity to reflect light) of a substant physical in the derivative sense of 'physical'; that substant being what an apple is in so far as perceivable only visually." [3] Such interpretation, of course, is never explicit, and the precise characterization of it is a matter of great detail.[4]

The same analysis that applies to sensation also applies to feelings and to mental acts. Take the former first. It makes sense to say both that I experience a tornado and that I experience a fear of it. Obviously, however, I do not experience them in the same way. I perceive the tornado, and I feel the fear. 'Perceiving the tornado' and 'feeling the fear' again refer to wholly different situations. The tornado is the object of my perceiving and exists independently of it, while fear is not the object of my feeling and does not exist independently of it. Fear is a kind of feeling and its whole *esse* consists in that feeling. Its *esse* is indeed its *experiri*.

By mental acts Ducasse means such activities as inferring, remembering, imagining, supposing, and so on. They are ways of *doing* something, unlike sensing, which is a way of *undergoing* something. They are to be contrasted with physical acts like walking, throwing, and pushing. Note that the proper contrast with 'mental act' is 'physical act' and not 'physical movement.' This point will become crucial soon.

3 *Ibid.*, p. 106.
4 *Nature, Mind, and Death*, pp. 304–53.

The point now is to see what distinction between the mental and physical can be made in this context. It turns out to be similar to—in fact, isomorphically identical with—the previous ones. A physical act is the object of perceiving in the same way that a physical object or a physical event, like a tornado, is and exists independently of such perception, while mental acts are not objects of perception and exist only insofar as they are operative. The *esse* of any mental act is its *operari*.

The nature of the present position, it should be clear, is that of interactionistic dualism. This fact follows not only from the definitions of 'mental' and 'physical' but also from the contrast between mental and physical acts. Physical acts like walking, throwing, and pushing are essentially different from physical movements like the falling of water or a rock. They are, in short, the results in part of mental acts (and in part of muscle contractions, etc.). Hence there is a causal interaction between mental and physical events. However, it is not a causal interaction between two substances in a substratum sense. There is no notion here of a mental or physical substance that undergoes changes or holds properties together. The only notion of physical substance is the common-sensical one in which glass, lead, and water, e.g., are called substances. They are substances in the sense that they are integrated sets of capacities. The substance lead, e.g., consists in the following integrated sets of capacities: fusibility, pliability, inelasticity, visibility, specific gravity 11.34, etc. To say that there is a substance that "possesses" these capacities would be like saying that a week is something over and above the seven days which make it up.[5]

The analysis of 'capacity,' in turn, is extremely detailed and depends upon the notion of causality.[6] There are six

[5] "Mind, Matter and Bodies," p. 105.

[6] Ducasse, "Substants, Capacities and Tendencies," *The Review of Metaphysics*, 18 (1964), pp. 23–37.

formal categories of capacities. (i) There is the capacity for *activity* of some particular kind, as an ivory ball, e.g., has the (intransitive) capacity of rolling. (ii) There is the capacity to be in a *state* of some particular kind, as liquid lead, e.g., has the capacity of acquiring solidity. (iii) There is the capacity of a substant S (Ducasse's term for "substance") to *affect* directly or indirectly a substant Z—indicated by such terms as "abrasiveness," "corrosiveness," and "toxicity." (When S is a purposive agent, then the instrument by which the effect is caused is an *act* and the effect intentionally caused a *deed*.) (iv) There is the capacity for a Substant Z to be affected directly or indirectly by a Substant S—indicated by such terms as "abradibility," "corrodibility," and "intoxicability." (v) There is the capacity for a Substant S to *endure* changes (the capacity of a knife, e.g., to become dull and sharp again while continuing throughout to be the same knife). (vi) There is, finally, the capacity of Substant S to *change into something generically different* (the capacity of water, e.g., to be changed into uncombined oxygen and hydrogen). Careful attention to the examples indicates that all six varieties of capacity depend upon the notion of *causality*, and hence the analysis of this concept again becomes crucial to the mind-body relationship.

The nature of the causal relation involved in causal interaction and in the analysis of 'capacity' must be defined in such a way that there is no puzzle about how physical events, which belong to the realm of space and time, and mental events, to which spatial notions are inapplicable, can ever causally interact—and in a way that there is no puzzle about how the same causal analysis can be given to both mental and physical substants. The definition of the causal relation which Ducasse gives is both non-Humean and non-metaphysical: "Causation . . . is the *triadic* relation which obtains between the three factors that together constitute an experiment. They are: 1) a concrete *state of affairs S* in which only two changes, whether simple or complex, occur; 2) one of these a change C occurring at a time T; and 3) the other a change E that begins to occur after change C has begun to occur. This triadic relation is *not* a *sign* that causation, in some mysterious sense, is occurring, but is *causation itself*, and is perceived by the performer or observer of a well-conducted experiment." [7] This definition, it is clear, is wholly neutral about the nature of the events which are supposedly causally related. The definition leaves open "whether the cause-event and the effect-event are both physical, or both psychical, or either one of them physical and the other psychical." The causality relation "requires only that both the cause and the effect be *events*." [8]

⌐ By way of summary: 'Mental' and 'physical' are irreducible concepts and each has a significantly different type of referent. The former has a connate accusative and the latter an alien accusative. Sensing is epistemically primary and the objects of perception ontologically primary. Mental and physical substants causally interact, and both types of substants are interpreted as integrated sets of capacities. Capacities are given a causal analysis—one which allows both for interaction and a similar analysis of mental and physical ⟨capacities.

2.

(i) Ducasse's analysis of 'sensation,' it should be clear, entails the falsity of the sense-data view. Sensing does not have an object but is itself a completely determinate way of experiencing. 'I sense bluely' is the correct locution rather than 'I sense blue.' There is, to be sure, a sense in which Ducasse does admit that sensations are objects of experience,

<hr>

[7] Ducasse, "Causation: Perceivable or Only Inferred?" *Philosophy and Phenomenological Research*, 26 (1965), p. 178.

[8] Ducasse, "Minds, Matter and Bodies," p. 85.

namely, when a person introspectively attends to his sensing. Introspection brings the bluely sensing from the periphery to the center of consciousness. But when sensing is attended to it does not become thereby the object of attending in the sense in which a chair is the object of perceptual attention. In the former case, attending is a mental act the object of which is a species of experiencing.

Advocates of a sense-data view generally believe that an ostensive definition of a sense-datum is possible—by referring, e.g., to a blue patch, speck, or line after-image seen with closed eyes. But such a procedure, Ducasse says, proves nothing.[9] No one denies the experiences indicated; the question at issue is whether to interpret them as species of sensing (or sensations) or as sense data which are objects of consciousness. The great difficulty with the latter interpretation is that sense data, it seems, then can appear to have characteristics they do not really have and can appear to exist when in fact they do not. But such a concept then becomes indistinguishable from that of a physical object or material thing and is a useless duplication of concepts. Moreover, it loses the original point of introducing the concept of sense data—sense data were presumably what were experienced in cases of illusion and hallucination. Ducasse concludes that " 'sense-data' and its synonyms 'sensa' and 'sensibles' are therefore treacherous words unless, in the case of what they designate, *reality consists in appearance, and appearance constitutes reality*. That is, unless, in *their* case, *esse est percipi*."[10]

(ii) Ducasse's analysis also entails the falsity of what might be called the sense-data view of feelings. According to this view, there is a nominative as well as an adverbial form of feeling words and the latter always presupposes the

9 *Ibid.*, pp. 107–108.
10 *Ibid.*, p. 90.

former—e.g., '*P* painfully feels pain.' On this view, feeling words refer not only to a species of experiencing but also to an object of experience. Since pain is a datum of experience it makes sense to say that John Smith "owns" a pain datum, no one else can "have" it, and so on.

There are various routes to this datum view of feelings, although, again, advocates of it seem to prefer the ostensive definition route. They refer to facts like this: an ordinary person experiences pain painfully while a masochist experiences it pleasantly—hence we must distinguish between pain as a datum of experience and pain as a way of experiencing. Such a procedure, again, proves nothing, however, for nobody denies the facts indicated. The question at issue is what constitutes the correct philosophical interpretation of the facts. That the above fact does not warrant the datum interpretation of feeling becomes clear, it seems to me, from the following considerations. One cannot generate the distinction if he limits himself to the experience of an ordinary person; here there is *prima facie* no difference between saying, "I am experiencing pain" and "I am experiencing painfully." To generate the distinction, then, one needs the masochist. But such a case has a completely different analysis than the ordinary one. Experiencing painfully in the case of the masochist is the partial cause of his subsequent pleasure, the rest of the cause being found in certain past events of his childhood. It is in cases like this that it is true to say that others can know a great deal more about a person's feelings than that person himself. Since the case of the masochist can be given a causal interpretation and the case of the ordinary person needs no interpretation other than the adverbial one, the sort of comparison which generates the datum view disappears and thus the need for the view along with it.

It is difficult to tell what ontological status is ascribed to the particulars called the "data of feelings." It is unclear whether or not they live a life of their own or are just as dependent upon the adverbial nature of experiencing as the latter is supposedly dependent on the nominative. If the former, then they are odd entities to introduce into the world; and if the latter, then they are unnecessary since the adverbial interpretation is sufficient to say all that needs to be said.

(iii) Ducasse's dualism avoids the deficiencies of that metaphysical dualism which maintains that Mind and Matter are fundamentally different substances between which no causal or conceptual connections are possible. The consequence of this view is that there can be no causal connection between a mental event and what we would ordinarily take to be its physical manifestation. There would be no causal connection, e.g., between my pain, on the one hand, and my screaming and writhing on the ground, on the other. It commits one to the following view of the meaning of mental words. Since there is only the sensation and no natural expression of it, the whole meaning of 'pain' comes simply from its associations with the instances of this type of sensation.

This type of dualism can be rejected on various grounds. It follows from this view that a person could not communicate with anyone when he used sensation and feeling words since no one else could know with what he had associated them. But clearly we do communicate about these matters. Hence this sort of dualism must be mistaken. Even worse, this view cannot even be intelligibly formulated without violating its own thesis about meaning. This sort of dualist cannot even talk about words being the names of sensations, since such a procedure uses the notion of sensations in their ordinary senses which, in turn, presupposes the natural expression of sensations. 'Pain,' e.g., has a use because a child learns to associate it with a certain sensation of his own in contexts of his own exclamations, withdrawals, writhings, and so on.

Ducasse's dualism avoids all of these difficulties for several reasons. First, his notion of interactionism is a commonsensical one and not a substantial dualism. Ducasse has no metaphysical concept of substance in the sense of a substratum that undergoes changes or holds properties together. He conceives substances, either mental or physical, as integrated sets of capacities of different sorts, and in order to avoid the misleading connotations of traditional views calls his own concept "substants" rather than "substances." Since he has no concept of substance in the traditional sense he has no problem of explaining how it is possible for two substances with incompatible natures to causally affect each other.

Second, Ducasse's view of causal interaction between mental and physical events allows him to say, e.g., that fear of a tornado caused him to run to the cellar, the feeling of pain caused him to say "Oh!" and suck his finger, etc., and thus to provide the contexts in which one learns the ordinary meanings of words like fear, pain, and all the others that philosophers appropriate, and hence to appreciate precisely the sort of use such terms have. Ducasse thus has no problem of explaining how it is that, in fact, people do communicate about matters of sensation and feeling. Communication is presupposed in his interactionism precisely because it entails the community and contextual view of the meanings of sensation and feeling words. I am not saying that Ducasse actually makes these points about communication and the meaning of sensation and feeling words. What I am claiming is that Ducasse's system contains nothing that runs counter to these claims—indeed gives the epistemic grounds for legitimately making them—and hence avoids the deficiencies of traditional dualism.

(iv) Ducasse's own concept of physical substant, it might be argued, is itself untenable. It seems strange to say that a physical substant is simply a set of capacities. After all, something has to have, or exhibit, such capacities.[11] Capacities do not exist in a vacuum. This criticism is a legitimate one and need not reflect any traditional view of substance as a substratum on the part of the critic. Such a critic might reject a phenomenalistic account of 'physical object,' but he would at least admit that such a view is intelligible. The meaning is clear anyway when someone says that a pencil is nothing more than what it is, or can be, experienced to be—a certain color, shape, hardness, capacity to make marks, and so on. But it is not at all clear what Ducasse has in mind when he says that a piece of lead, as a physical substant, is simply a collection of capacities like fusibility, pliability, specific gravity 11.34, and so on. Something has to have or exhibit these capacities.

However, this difficulty over the notion of substant evaporates as soon as one notices that for Ducasse 'visibility' counts as a capacity for a physical substant. By calling visibility a capacity here he means that a piece of lead has the capacity, under certain conditions, to cause a certain visual sensation. For him, the lead, which is the referent of a perception in which there is always an element of interpretation and (unconscious) inference, is what has all the above capacities—including the capacity of producing those sensations by which it becomes known.

(v) Ducasse's view successfully avoids the vagaries of the perenially popular double-aspect solution to the mind-body problem. The notion that mind and body are two "aspects"

[11] *Ibid.*, pp. 99, 104–105.

of one identical thing is wholly metaphorical and will remain so until the proponents of this doctrine can identify that entity or substance of which brain and mind are supposed to be "aspects." The ordinary notion of 'aspect' is perfectly clear. The aspects of something are what one sees when one looks at the thing from different vantage points. Or, more broadly, the aspects of anything are whatever experiences are caused in an observer of a physical object, no matter what their nature. One might, e.g., refer to the visible, audible, or tactual aspects of a bird. Still more broadly, 'aspect' might be intended to designate the various kinds of questions that can be asked without incongruity about a given entity. But in all these cases, however different, there is always inherently a reference to something which *has,* but *is not itself,* any of its sensible or rational aspects. Conversely, nothing can *be* an aspect unless there is some entity of which it is an aspect. And it is at this point that the proponents of the double-aspect theory depart from any sensible use of 'aspect' because they never successfully identify the entity of which brain and mind are supposedly simply two different aspects.

Sometimes it is suggested that the body itself or the brain is the needed entity or substance, and that mental activity *is* brain activity but "viewed from within." (Compare this version of the double-aspect theory with the later identity theory.) But this so-called refinement of the theory is really no help at all, for it simply amounts to another unexplained metaphor. The claim is that physiologists know the brain from the "outside" but that everyone knows the brain from the "inside" as mental activity. The simple metaphor which suggests this claim is clear: it is like looking at a house from the outside and looking at the identically same house from the inside. Certainly things look different but it is the same house. Unfortunately the proponents of this view leave the nature or manner of the similarity between the two cases unspecified—and, indeed, it is difficult to see, upon reflection, what similarity could conceivably appear. And if the person who makes the claim of similarity cannot describe the special way of knowing the brain from the inside, "the reason is not that no words exist in English wherewith to do so, but that no clear idea, if any idea at all, exists in him as to the nature of that alleged way of knowing; so that 'viewing from within' (as applied to the brain) is then only a fancy name for ignorance of anything going on in the brain other than what physiology describes." [12]

(vi) It should be pointed out that while Ducasse's dualism entails the falsity of materialistic views like the recent identity theory it does not entail the falsity of every sense of 'materialism.' One sense of this term is compatible with his position.

(a) The identity theorist is impressed by the fact that two different referring phrases can nevertheless have the identically same referent. They apply this to the mind-body problem by saying that statements about mental states and statements about brain states are different in meaning but nevertheless have the identically same brain state as referent. The identity theorist believes that the scientific explainability of mental states in terms of brain states is the criterion for claiming that a mental state and the brain state invariably accompanying it are one and the same thing.

Ducasse's emphasis on the intentional nature of mental and physical acts, as distinct from movements, however, helps one to see the deficiencies of this form of materialism. Brain states in principle could never explain the intentional aspects of actions. The identity theorist might reply: I ad-

[12] Ducasse makes this point in correspondence. Cf. Ducasse, *A Critical Examination of the Belief in a Life After Death* (Springfield, Illinois: Charles C. Thomas Publisher, 1961), pp. 71–73.

mit that there is a difference between the movement of a human body (it falls) and an action (he jumps down) but insist that both references are to the same physical movement—they differ only in *concept*. The critic need not deny this but would in turn insist that there could then be no microscopic information about brain states which could explain the difference either between the concept of a movement and the concept of an action or between the concept of anything and the thing itself.

The identity theorist, I suspect, is misled in the following way. It seems clear to him that common salt and sodium chloride, lightning and electrical discharge, etc., are simply different ways of referring to the same thing, or identical state of affairs. Hence, he concludes that since molar-micro physical states are identical, he has the right to assume, unless he is shown convincing evidence to the contrary, that mental states and brain states, as molar and micro, respectively, are identical. However, it appears that the allegedly clear-cut examples of common salt-sodium chloride, lightning-electrical discharge, and so on being identical are not as convincing as they appear at first sight. For in the molar half of all such alleged identities there appears to be an implicit reference to sensing, and hence to mental states. The problem thus appears in all macro-micro examples and not only in the case of mental states and brain states. Hence the identity supposedly existing in the former cannot be used as a bridge to make plausible an identity in the latter.

(b) There is, however, one materialistic viewpoint which is compatible with Ducasse's dualism. This view is that mental and brain states are not numerically identical but that between the two states there is a one-to-one correspondence of elements in which every mental state has a brain state as its cause. Ducasse, in fact, considers such a position not only logically possible but as having some evidence in its favor.[13] However, he apparently thinks that evidence for the independent existence of mental states is slightly stronger and so seems to reject even this sort of materialism. It would be perfectly possible for someone else, though, to be a materialist in the present sense and share all the rest of Ducasse's views on perception and the mind-body problem that we have been discussing.

(vii) Finally, it should be pointed out that Ducasse's analysis of 'causality' is compatible with but not required by his views on perception and the mind-body relation. All that is required of one holding his views is that he not hold a view of causality which makes interaction a mystery. Ducasse's view of causality nicely meets this requirement but so does the Humean view and, as far as I can see, even the entailment view. The only view of causality eliminated by the present analysis of 'mental' and 'physical' seems to be the "activity" interpretation.

---

[13] *Nature, Mind, and Death,* Part IV.

VI

Strawson's Concept of a Person

by Dwight Van de Vate, Jr.

1) Meaning and Use: Two Analogies.

I have two purposes in these comments on Professor Strawson's article, "Persons." [1] I take it that producing an account of the concept of a person is the main problem of the

Dwight Van de Vate, Jr. was educated at Wesleyan and Yale (Ph.D., 1956) and has taught at the University of Mississippi, Florida State University, and Memphis State University. He is currently Professor of Philosophy at The University of Tennessee. Formerly Co-Editor of *The Southern Journal of Philosophy*, he is formerly treasurer and currently president-elect of the Southern Society for Philosophy and Psychology, and author of several articles.

[1] This article was originally published in *Minnesota Studies in the Philosophy of Science*, Vol. II, *Concepts, Theories, and the Mind-Body Problem*, ed. Herbert Feigl, Michael Scriven, and Grover Maxwell (Minneapolis: University of Minnesota Press, 1958), pp. 330–353. It has been included in at least three anthologies: *The Philosophy of Mind*,

philosophy of mind. I want to show how Strawson's account of the concept of a person depends on a misleading analogy. My purpose in showing this is to present an alternative analogy and at the same time to argue for a broader perspective on the philosophy of mind. It will be helpful if I sketch out my own position in advance.[2]

Strawson asks, "How is the concept of a person possible?" (148) He wants to know "what it is in the natural facts that makes it intelligible that we should have this concept" (148). To "have" a concept means to use it: "we"—presumably Strawson means "each of us"—"operate conceptual schemes" (151), the concept has "employment" (150). Strawson is guided by Wittgenstein's well-known analogy: concepts are like tools, like the instruments we use to accomplish our purposes. We "do things with words" and their meanings. To show how we do things with words, we compare them to "a hammer, pliers, a saw, a screwdriver, a rule, a glue-pot,

---

ed. V. C. Chappell (Englewood Cliffs, N. J.: Prentice-Hall, 1962), pp. 127–146; *Essays in Philosophical Psychology,* ed. Donald F. Gustafson (Anchor Books edition; Garden City, N. Y.: Doubleday, 1964), pp. 377–403; *Wittgenstein and the Problem of Other Minds,* ed. Harold Morick (New York: McGraw-Hill, 1967), pp. 127–153. A revised and expanded version appears as Chapter 3, "Persons," in Strawson's book, *Individuals: An Essay in Descriptive Metaphysics* (Anchor Books edition; Garden City, N. Y.: Doubleday, 1963; originally published in London by Methuen & Co., Ltd., 1959). Because the argument of the revised version does not differ in any essential way from the argument of the original article, and because the latter is accessible in so many places, I have drawn all my direct quotations from the original article. Page references—in parentheses—are to Morick. All italics in quotations are Strawson's.

2 The interested reader may refer also to "Other Minds and the Uses of Language," *American Philosophical Quarterly,* Vol. III, No. 3 (July, 1966), pp. 250–254; "Disagreement as a Dramatic Event," *The Monist,* Vol. 49, No. 2 (April, 1965), pp. 248–261; "The Genesis of Privacy," *J. of Existentialism,* Vol. VII, No. 26 (Winter, 1966/67), pp. 233–242; "Laughter and Detachment," *Southern J. of Phil.,* Vol. III, No. 4 (Winter, 1965), pp. 163–171; "Violence and Persons," *The Philosophy Forum,* Vol. VII, No. 3 (March, 1969), pp. 3–31.

glue, nails and screws"—the list of PI 11. To clarify a concept, to give an account of it, we show what job we do with
it: like a tool, a concept is defined by its function.

Of course this is only an analogy. Words, concepts, sentences, and propositions aren't *really* tools. For example, a
tool will be owned by someone, but no one can own a word.
The analogy is useful, though, for each of us uses these conceptual entities as means to his various ends, and, like a tool,
a given means may be well or ill adapted to a given end. The
analogy reminds us, among other things, that the meaning of
a word is often not sharply defined, but covers a range of
possible uses, some obvious and efficient, some obscure and
cumbersome.

The "tool" analogy is not the only possible analogy. We
also do things with parliaments, courts, licensing authori-
ties, systems of weights and measures, and codes of etiquette. Institutions such as these are *public* tools. When we
say "we use them," "we" doesn't mean "each of us individually," but "all of us collectively." The purposes we accomplish by means of them are first of all public purposes, and
only afterward the private purposes of individuals.

Now I shall argue that the actual use we make of the
concept of a person is better clarified by comparing the concept to a public institution with a collective purpose than
by comparing it to a tool with a private purpose. I begin
with an emphatic phenomenological "look and see." The concept of a person is a noun-concept. Any noun-concept divides
the world into two classes: the things to which it correctly
applies and the things to which it doesn't apply. We use the
concept of a person to divide the world into persons and other
things—hereafter I shall call them simply "things." Considered with old-fashioned empirical honesty, this language-
game is eminently practical and serious. We think of persons (even—indeed, especially—when we abuse them) as

the most privileged and significant of beings. Their status logically, morally, and legally is absolutely superior to the status of things. Only persons may correct one another's reasoning. Only persons may be morally self-determining. Only persons have legal rights and obligations. Our actions are defined fundamentally by persons, only derivatively by things.

The distinction of persons from things is the most fundamental of social institutions. Society exists only in its members. It depends absolutely on their ability to recognize one another, for each must be aware that one set of rules applies to persons, another set to things. Therefore the ability to distinguish persons from things is the ability earliest inculcated in children and most harshly required of adults. We train children to distinguish persons from things automatically, unthinkingly. We want making the distinction to become the most deeply engrained and spontaneous of their habits. We may call this training "the socialization process." Persons are its products. We socialize our children so that they too will become persons, for the socialization process is not infallible: we will deny the privilege of being a person to the adult who displays an insufficient socialization.

Now according to Strawson (and many other philosophers), there are "natural facts" which make it intelligible that we should have our concept of a person. Our concept corresponds to something "out there," it singles out a class of beings which are naturally distinguished from things by a property, the property of being self-conscious. The socialization process doesn't create these self-conscious persons, it modifies them. They are self-conscious to begin with, and by socializing them, we merely give them more attractive selves to be conscious of. We can refer to persons with our concept of a person because there "are" persons in the same sense in which there "are" mountains and there "are" galactic nebulae—in the sense, namely, that they *are* whether we refer to them or not. And here "we" means "each of us," since the idea that we might refer to something collectively is not so much unintelligible as it is morally repugnant (150–151).

I argue to the contrary that persons are not "natural facts" at all, but social facts which arise in self-conscious opposition to the natural facts. The natural fact which persons are created by self-consciously opposing is the human body. Persons are "out there" because we collectively put them "out there" by socializing them, by training them to control their bodies. We enforce a system of conventional ways of interfering with the natural behavior of the body, a system of conventional modes of self-control. Each of us will perceive what exhibits the self-control required by these conventions to be a person, entitled to all the privileges and significance of that status. What falls short one will perceive to be less than a person: one cannot allow it to correct him, nor insult him, nor attack his causes at law.

One cannot allow this, for were one to do so, others would think one insufficiently socialized, and one would forfeit one's own person status. A child can talk to his teddy bear with impunity, but a child is not yet a person. An adult who really talks to teddy, who really thinks—or permits others to think that he thinks—that teddy is lonesome, will not long be at liberty to manage his own affairs. Society rests on force in the sense that if the individual person does not grant person status to those who deserve it, he will lose it himself. Thus being a person is a *reciprocal* affair: one grants person status to what one recognizes has granted person status to oneself; and to accept person status from another entails granting that status to him also. The dependence of the individual person on others is absolute: his being as a person is conferred on him by them. At the same time, however, each of them is equally dependent upon him.

The reciprocity of person status is repeated in the more concrete roles persons play: the mother must have a child, the hero a villain, the trusted adviser someone who trusts his advice. These social roles are the means by which persons locate one another in time and space and perceive one another. In other words, persons perceive one another by interacting with one another, responding to one another's cues, apportioning time and space among themselves by mutually agreeing what each is trying to be. Where this agreement fails, persons must reidentify one another until they do agree. This is a logical "must." If we do not agree what each of us is trying to be, our acts will be meaningless. If I am to be a man of extraordinary refinement, someone else must be willing to play the clod. If no one ever is, if the gestures of superior sensibility I privately rehearse are never publicly accepted, then if I insist on them enough, my claims to refinement will be thought hallucinatory, "out of contact." Someone who cannot recognize who he himself is cannot recognize who others are either. They cannot grant him person status, for they cannot interact with him.

Now a thing has just those properties which, in the ideal long run, we all agree it has. In this sense, a thing might be said to be characterized by mutual agreement, by how we agree to talk *about* it. A person, however, is characterized by how we agree to talk to him—which will be determined by how we expect him to talk back, to reciprocate. It seems strange to say we perceive persons by interacting with them. We philosophers are accustomed to saying we don't perceive persons at all, but rather their bodies. That is why it is important to point out that the question whether or not a body is the body of a (living) person has the gravest practical consequences, both for the thing (person) in question and for its (his) questioners. If a body is (the body of) a person, then I ought to treat it one way, if not I may treat it differently; and I had better know the difference, for persons are very special, and very dangerous. But when is a body a person? [3] What is the "criterial behavior" for being a person? I take it that whatever it is, the reciprocity of person status will be the key to it, that is, it will be just that form of behavior which others require in order themselves to be persons. That is why the "marginally functional person," who is psychotic or retarded or a felon or senile, who looks almost like a person, but whom nevertheless we cannot perceive as a person and permit all the privileges of a person (such as running around on the loose), is such an important and (to my mind) neglected philosophical topic. He has a body, but—not the way persons have bodies. Why? Surely because the way he has his body threatens the way persons have their bodies. He cannot restrain himself: he might assault them or undress in front of them or steal from them, etc. What these forms of misbehavior elucidate is their common opposite: the self-control that we collectively demand of persons because we individually must depend upon one another.

"The human body," writes Wittgenstein, "is the best picture of the human soul." [4] This is hyperbole. The human body is the *only* picture of the human soul, that is, one is a person by *not* being a thing, by restraining one's hostilities, controlling one's eliminative impulses, covering one's limbs with clothing, and holding oneself upright. These forms of self-control are the behavioral idiom that permits us to tell

---

[3] I have benefited from the excellent discussion of Douglas C. Long, "The Philosophical Concept of a Human Body," *Phil. Rev.*, Vol. LXXIII, No. 3 (July, 1964), pp. 321–337.

[4] *Philosophical Investigations*, p. 178.

one another we have selves. Philosophers have been slow to study them and slower still to study their opposites, for philosophy is carried on in seminar rooms, among the more decorous and well-defined of social places. Mere presence in the seminar room is almost certain evidence of good socialization, and when that evidence is buttressed by others' good humor and good manners, the result seems logically necessary. "I know for sure what I am thinking, but I cannot be sure what you are thinking," one says. But I am certain that you are not thinking of assaulting me or I would prepare to defend myself rather than sitting here debating with you. We can ignore the fact that each of us is a person because he constantly promises the others that he will not do violence to them (and they accept his promise), for it is a tautology that nothing like violence is supposed to happen in the seminar room.

No one knows to what extent failure to reflect on the nature of philosophy as a specialized form of social activity has affected the philosophy of mind. But if certain concepts— by far the most important is the concept of a person—are like public tools or public institutions, then to clarify these concepts will be to show how they contribute to the stability and self-maintenance of society, that is, how they make everyday social life possible. Such a "functionalistic" clarification must be dialectically adequate. It must also guard against the limitations of the seminar room perspective. It must show not only how the concept of a person is used after the fact, as it were, in decorous, well-defined social situations, but also how it is used, and far more fundamentally used, to define situations which are ill-defined, threatening, embarrassing, messy, illogical.

In these introductory remarks, I have tried to sketch out the point of view from which I criticize Strawson. I ought to say that my criticism of Strawson can be looked upon as an extension of the Strawsonian perspective. Like Strawson, I take the concept of a person to be "logically primitive." But I differ from Strawson regarding *how* the concept is logically primitive. Strawson contends, as we shall see, that certain highly general facts of nature make it possible for us to regard both mind and body as abstractions from the concrete entity which is the person. I contend, on the other hand, that the concept of a person is logically primitive in the sense that persons are related to one another by a reciprocity which is not analyzable into any concatenation of natural facts—which is, indeed, a social fact, or the fact of society itself. Since to me, "person" means "member of society," it could be said that Strawson takes the concept of the individual person to be logically primitive and I take the concept of society to be logically primitive.

2) *The Strawsonian Account.*

Strawson asks, "Why are one's states of consciousness ascribed to the very same thing as certain corporeal characteristics, a certain physical situation, etc.? And once this question is raised, another question follows it, viz: Why are one's states of consciousness ascribed to (said to be of, or to belong to) anything at all?" (128–129) It seems to be a feature of our concept of a person that we ascribe to a person both conscious experiences and corporeal characteristics. Strawson wants to show what makes this concept possible.

One might hold our concept confused. This is the position of Cartesian dualists, also of the upholders, if any, of what Strawson calls the "no-ownership" or "no-subject" theory of the self. According to the latter, the subject of experiences is the body, that is, experiences are "had" by the body by being causally dependent on the body; but there is no ego to provide experience with a unity or integrity beyond what is given it by causally depending on a single body. The difficulty with this theory is that the sense of possession or ownership the theory claims to analyze away must be used to state the theory itself: "All *my* experiences depend on the state of a certain body." This dependence is supposed to be causal, and therefore contingent. But it cannot be contingent unless experiences can be identified as mine independently of their causal dependence on a certain body—which is just what the theory denies. "States, or experiences, one might say, *owe* their identity as particulars to the identity of the persons whose states or experiences they are. . . . The requirements of identity rule out logical transferability of ownership" (134). All my experiences, in other words, are *necessarily* mine: ". . . it does not seem to make sense to suggest, for example, that the identical pain which was in fact one's own might have been another's" (134).

Strawson continues, ". . . it is a necessary condition of one's ascribing states of consciousness, experiences, to oneself, in the way one does, that one should also ascribe them (or be prepared to ascribe them) to others who are not oneself" (136). But how is this empathy, this ability to put oneself in the other person's place, to see the world through his eyes, possible? One experiences one's own states of consciousness immediately, non-inferentially. How, then, is this empathy possible, in the face of the familiar privacy problem?

Certainly it is *not* possible if others are identifiable only as Cartesian egos (to which only private experiences can be ascribed), for then it would have to be grounded on the argument from analogy. I should have to reason that because I observe certain relations to obtain between my body-subject and my ego-subject, that therefore analogous relations must obtain between others' body-subjects (which I can identify) and their ego-subjects (which I cannot identify, and so cannot legitimately import to provide the analogy with its fourth term) (138).

"What we have to acknowledge," Strawson concludes, "in order to begin to free ourselves from these difficulties, is the *primitiveness* of the concept of a person. What I mean by the concept of a person is the concept of a type of entity such that *both* predicates ascribing states of consciousness *and* predicates ascribing corporeal characteristics, a physical situation, etc., are equally applicable to a single individual of that single type" (138).

"Primitive" means "unanalyzable." Thus Strawson's thesis is that it is a necessary condition of our having our concept of a person that a person not be analyzable into a pure ego and a body, but instead that these two subjects themselves be analytic discriminates from the single entity which is the person. Predicates implying the possession of states of consciousness ("P-predicates") are ascribed to the same thing to which a physical situation, weight, etc. ("M-predicates"), are ascribed. If indeed P-predicates and M-predicates are to have the same logical status, be of the same logical type, then the rules for ascribing P-predicates must (at least in part) be identical to the rules for ascribing M-predicates. "After all," Strawson writes confidently, "there is no difficulty about distinguishing bodies from one another, no difficulty about identifying bodies" (137). Hence there must be ". . . in principle some way of telling, with regard to any individual . . . and any P-predicate, whether that individual possesses that P-predicate. And, in the case of at least some P-predicates, the ways of telling must constitute in some sense logically adequate kinds of criteria for the ascription of the P-predicate" (142), for otherwise we shall be back to Cartesianism again. Thus P-predicates must be (in general) other-ascribable on the basis of the observation of behavior and self-ascribable *not* on the basis of the observation of behavior: "If there were no concepts answering to the characterization I have just given, we should have no philosophical problem about the soul; but equally we should not have *our* concept of a person" (145).

"The fact that we find it natural to individuate as persons the members of a certain class of what might also be individuated as organic bodies does not mean that such a conceptual scheme is inevitable for any class of beings not utterly unlike ourselves" (150). Thus there might be intelligent hymenopterous insects (my example) who would have a use for the plurals "we" and "they", but not for the singulars "you," "I," and "he"—who would behave, in other words, as if they were members of a single individual, not themselves individuals. "The point I wish to make is that a condition for the existence, the use, of the concept of an individual person is that this should happen *only sometimes*" (151).

Strawson's next two sentences are especially worth noting: "It is absolutely useless to say, at this point: But all the same, even if this happened all the time, every member of the group would have an individual consciousness, would be an individual subject of experience. The point is, once more, that there is no sense in speaking of the individual consciousness just as such, for there is no way of identifying such pure entities" (151). He adds in a footnote, "More accurately: their identification is necessarily secondary to the identification of persons."

When we say, "All my experiences are necessarily mine," the "I" or "ego" which "owns" one's experiences is what is sometimes called the "subject" of experience, that which does the knowing, as opposed to that which is known, the "object." The fact that one must so overwork the double apostrophe to discuss the subject indicates how mysterious, indeed, "metaphysical," it is. While on the one hand it seems paradoxical to deny its existence—thought without a thinker is like a walk taking itself—on the other hand, it obviously cannot experience itself. One wants to say: manifestly it cannot manifest itself. Were it to do so, it must do so in an experience of some sort, this experience in turn must have an owner, and now it seems one is trying to stand behind one's own back. An unexperienceable entity has no place in an empiricist philosophy. So when Hume looked into himself, he never found an ego-substance, only perceptions. Kant realized that "the pure ego" is a name for something, viz., the unity of experience; but this something is a formal or analytic unity, not a mysterious metaphysical substance. Perhaps Wittgenstein means the same when he says there "is" no such thing as the pure ego, also that it is not part of the world, but its limit.

> So, then, the word 'I' never refers to this, the pure subject. But this does not mean, as the no-ownership theorist must think and as Wittgenstein, at least at one period, seemed to think, that 'I' in some cases does not refer at all. It refers, because I am a person among others. And the predicates which would, *per impossibile*, belong to the pure subject if it could be referred to, belong properly to the person to which 'I' does refer (140).

Thus for Strawson, an individual person arises at the intersection of a principle of unity—the ego—and a principle of differentiation—the body—but both are analytic discriminates or abstractions from the single entity which is the person, rather than substances in their own right. The word "I," one might say, can't refer *only* to my body, for the connection of *my* experiences with me is logically prior to the contingent, causal connections of my experiences with my body: my experiences are necessarily mine. But equally the word "I" can't refer only to the pure ego, for one pure ego is indistinguishable from another, and "I" refers to me as one person among others. So in order to provide "I" with the sort of reference it actually has (what Strawson is doing is "descriptive metaphysics"), we say that the concept of a person is primitive, meaning by this that a person is the sort of thing to which one ascribes both M-predicates and P-predicates, and meaning further that P-predicates are such as to be self-ascribed on one basis and other-ascribed on a different basis.

3) M-predicates and P-predicates: How to Weigh 150 lbs.

I think several features of this account should arouse one's suspicions. First, once Strawson has specified that M-predicates are to be ascribable to persons, they seem thereafter to drop out of the argument, the balance of it being confined largely to P-predicates. There is, after all, "no difficulty about identifying bodies." Second, to have both an M-description and a P-description is one logical feature of persons, while to have a P-description on one basis in the first-person case and on another basis in the third-person case is another and a different logical feature of persons. While there is the connection between them that third-person P-predicates are ascribed on the basis of behavior, that is, of M-descriptions, nevertheless these do seem to be distinct logical features, and to wrap them both up in the single word "primitive" seems at best hasty.

Where does the trouble lie? I take it that if I were to say, "Henry weighs 150 lbs.," this would be to ascribe an M-predicate to Henry—I might say the same, after all, of a block of marble or a carcass in the butcher's shop. To ascribe an M-predicate or corporeal characteristic to something is to give a physical description of it, the sort of description answerable to physicist's standards of accuracy. How one intends a description is determined, surely, by how one would respond if someone else challenged it. "You're wrong! He really weighs a little more than that." Now if I really mean to describe Henry's actual weight, I might undertake a lengthy series of measurements, determining it, let us say, to the nearest hundredth of an ounce. I could do the same for the carcass or the block of marble. I take it that then I could ascribe a weight to Henry with real authority, an authority I didn't have before I made my measurements.

If I handle the measuring process tactfully, no doubt Henry will be amused by my results. He should care what he weighs to the nearest hundredth of an ounce! And just what is Henry?

A person. And what is that? Following Strawson, something which has P-predicates, i.e. conscious states, i.e. (still following Strawson) what *I* have. I am interacting with Henry, *therefore* or *by that means* I credit Henry with what I have, consciousness. But persons never interact just as persons—the classification is too abstract, it doesn't provide sufficient clues to how each ought to act. Persons interact by playing particular social roles which identify them as to age, sex, social class, occupation, etc., thus sorting out what each owes to each. One cannot act (even malevolently) unless one knows how one ought to act, in other words, it is the social situation which gives an action its meaning, its intelligible structure, the social situation being mutually defined by the persons who are parties to it.

So we may suppose that Henry and I are co-workers in the laboratory making up the report of our measurements determining his weight: let this be the social situation, the basis on which we are interacting. Laboratory colleagues are supposed to take a special attitude—we familiarly speak of "objectivity," "detachment," etc.—towards the results of experiments. This attitude is part of the definition of the laboratory situation, that is, laboratory colleagues require it from and promise it to one another, and regard lapses from it as shameful. Henry interacts with me, then, on the basis of an implied promise that, whatever may be the outcome of the experiment, it isn't going to get to him. Our relationship will be unaffected by whatever his weight turns out to be.

Tautologically, Henry-to-me is whatever dangles at the other end of our relationship. If there be such a person as Henry-in-himself or Henry-to-God, *I* certainly cannot assert that there is anything but Henry-to-me. In other words, if I really think I am interacting with Henry, then I will refuse to distinguish among Henry-to-me, Henry-in-himself, and Henry-to-God. Just as I know that the face I turn toward Henry is determined by all that I am (most of which is none of Henry's business), so I will define Henry as much by what I don't know about him (but might) as by what I do know about him.

I forgot to mention something about Henry. He is seven feet, six inches tall. "Did you realize you only weigh 150 lbs.? My God, man, you look like a Giacometti!" My remark affects Henry's ability to interact with me. He must react to it. He knows I will count whatever he does as a reaction to it, even if he ignores it and does nothing at all. For example, if he does nothing, I might take him to be advertising his scientific detachment, to be showing me that he is more faithful to the laboratory proprieties than I am.

The body Henry has is the body he knows he has, the body whose features enter into the determination of his ability to interact with others. Features of his body apparent only to the specialized observer (his very exact weight, the shape of his appendix, the number of hairs on his head) are features of the body *he* has only in so far as they have a bearing on the features he is aware of and knows he has to react to, to "control." He has a weight, but not (in this sense) a mean weight of 150.003 lbs. He knows how to weigh about 150: he is supposed to make wry (and really rather annoying) remarks about his appearance to show that he's not self-conscious (even though it's obvious that he is) ; or he is supposed to have a brusque, withdrawn manner to show that he doesn't care what you say about him (even though it's obvious he cares) ; or he is supposed to smile too hard and flap like a scarecrow to show he doesn't mind cutting a ridiculous figure (even though it's obvious that he minds) ; or there are other possibilities. There are a number of methods for him to weigh about 150, methods by which he communicates to others that he knows he has (a particular sort of) body, so that therefore he can be trusted to respect their (particular sorts of) bodies; but there is no method for weighing exactly 150.003.

How does a body get to be the body *of a person?* If, following Strawson, we say that a "person" is what has *both* conscious states *and* a body, then evidently one can have the body of a person only by having the conscious states *of a person*. What makes this point tricky is that we have been trained to take the body—two arms, two legs, one head, one trunk, moving, breathing, etc.—as such a firmly established symbol for the mind, for the presence of a person, that we assume the symbol functions automatically and infallibly, "by nature," as it were. Given *that* kind of body (moving, breathing, etc.), there simply can't be any real (as opposed to metaphysical) doubt that one is in the presence of a mind, of something which has the conscious states of a person. I urge to the contrary that the body is not naturally given as an infallible symbol or evidence of the presence of the mind, but is made into such a symbol by the person who "has" it. The symbol works almost infallibly in laboratory or seminar room situations, but to say this is to say something tautological: the very presence of a body in social situations defined as these are defined is a sufficient guarantee that some person is making the right moves with it.

If one considers a messier social situation, however, this infallibility vanishes before one's eyes. Suppose Henry—

we may as well use him—has had a stroke. He opens his eyes: he's not dead! Is he still a person? Does he still have the conscious states of a person? Does he still, in other words, have what I have? That depends entirely on what he does, and it is easy to imagine him doing things which will disqualify him from being a person. If he just twitches and stares vacantly off into space, then I won't credit him with what I have. If he grins foolishly and exposes himself (an entertaining idiom), will I treat him then as if he had the consciousness appropriate to a person? Does he then have what I have, so that he is entitled to run around on the loose, etc.?

What weighs about 150—by acting as if he weighed about 150—is what, because it acts in this *appropriate* way, can be identified as Henry, who can then be found to have an exact weight of 150.003. Thus if what weighs 150.003 doesn't behave as if it weighs about 150, if its behavior is grossly inappropriate, if it insists that it has no body (being dead) or that its body is made of garbage, then it can't be our old friend and colleague Henry. Then the statement, "Henry weighs 150 lbs.," will lack a subject. Hence when one ascribes to this denotable person, Henry, the predicate "weighs 150 lbs.," one implies that Henry realizes what a handicap his unfortunate height-to-weight ratio is. To be a person with a body—rather than something less privileged and less significant—one has to display one's awareness that others too are persons with bodies, bodies in relation to which one has one's own body. Because it implies the presence of a conscious state, "weighs 150 lbs." must be a P-predicate, not an M-predicate. And so it doesn't help to say that a person is that to which we ascribe both M- and P-predicates, for what Strawson takes to be M-predicates ("weighs ten stone," "is in the drawing room") are really P-predicates. Only *after* having ascribed P-predicates to a person can we be in a position to ascribe M-predicates to him. (Strawson himself is aware that there may be a type ambiguity here. Cf. 142.) "Ascribe" is ambiguous. We ascribe predicates to persons by interacting with them. We don't interact with things, but we observe them by interacting with one another *about* them.

Strawson speaks of the M-predicate—P-predicate distinction as "a rough division" (141). But in what, to me at least, are the climactic pages of the article (138–140), he seems to suggest that the two halves of the division perform quite different functions in the general economy of the concept of a person. It is, he argues, "a necessary condition of states of consciousness being ascribed at all . . . that they should be ascribed to the *very same things* as certain corporeal characteristics, a certain physical situation, etc." (139). Why? Because if we start with the concept of a person as a compound of two subjects—an ego and a body—then as we examine the concept more closely, the ego inevitably begins to disappear from it. "For there could never be any question of assigning an experience, as such, to any subject other than oneself; and therefore never any question of assigning it to a subject at all" (139). Since the pure ego has no characteristics, and since each of us knows that he is necessarily different from anyone else, the burden of differentiating us from one another has to be thrown over onto the body, one's connection with one's body has to be made logically necessary, and hence the concept of a person as something to which both M- and P-predicates are ascribed has to be taken to be logically primitive. But, as I have tried to show, M-predicates simply will not support this burden, for before they can be ascribed to persons, persons must be *already differentiated* by P-predicates.

In another way of putting it, let us say Strawson wants to account for the fact that each person knows himself to be a single, self-identical thing. One recalls Butler's famous principle of self-identity, "Everything is what it is and not another thing." In a Cartesian humor, one could say that if one knows a particular thing, then one must know it clearly and distinctly: clearly, in that one knows (that it is) what it is; distinctly, in that one knows what it is not (i.e., that it is not another thing), and is therefore not apt to confuse it with other things. The distinction of M- from P-predicates can be looked upon as an attempt to clarify these two moments separately. Thus when one knows a person through his P-predicates (and that is what communicating with him is all about), then one knows what he is, or one knows him clearly. When one knows him through his M-predicates, then one knows what he is not, or one knows him distinctly. There are thus two moments, one of self-identity, the other of differentiation. But to say with Strawson that the concept of a person is "logically primitive" is merely to weld these two moments together by main force. And this can't work, for the two moments imply one another. To be oneself and not to be someone else can't be two distinct features of a single entity, features whose distinctness can be spelled out by two distinct lists of predicates. Instead, each feature simply means the other, i.e., they are really one feature.

4) The Pure Ego.

We introduced the pure ego into philosophy in order to provide a referent for the pronoun "I." But, says Strawson, once we acknowledge that the concept of a person is logically primitive, the temptation to countenance such a bizarre principle disappears.

> In particular, the problem that seems to have perplexed Hume does not exist—the problem of the principle of unity, of identity, of the particular consciousness, of the particular subject of 'perceptions' (experiences) considered as a primary particular. If there were

such a principle, then each of us would have to apply it in order to decide whether any contemporary experience of his was his or someone else's; and there is no sense in this suggestion (152–153).

I urge to the contrary that there is a great deal of sense in this suggestion, and to see what that sense is, is to see into the heart of the problem. I *can* reject, disclaim, disown my own contemporary experiences. (I shall come to a qualification in a moment.) They may be too much for me, they may overwhelm me, I may be simply incapable of assimilating them. I may then refuse to acknowledge them, I may say— and mean—"This cannot be happening," "This must be happening to someone else." Of course (this is the qualification), if others catch me out in this refusal, I will be forced to forfeit my right to be a person. They cannot trust me to pass judgment on how they take responsibility for their experiences if I am incapable of taking responsibility for my own. I might be said to have forfeited my right to refer to myself as "I," in the sense that, after I have been legally declared mentally incompetent, others will be entitled to take my first-person reports as symptoms of my derangement rather than as genuine messages.

Concerning the ontological argument, Kant remarks

> If, in an identical proposition, I reject the predicate while retaining the subject, contradiction results; and I therefore say that the former belongs necessarily to the latter. But if we reject subject and predicate alike, there is no contradiction; for nothing is then left that can be contradicted (A594 = B622, Smith's translation).

Similarly, *granted* that I have a creditable self to attach experiences to, then necessarily all my experiences are mine— that is a mere tautology. But it is *not* logically necessary that I have a creditable self, nor that "my experiences" (so to speak) belong to anyone at all. In the context of a philosophical discussion, one's self is a *fait accompli*: If one hadn't had a creditable self to present to one's fellow discussants, one couldn't have entered the discussion in the first place. In context, "I have a creditable self" or "I have indeed an 'I' " seems logically necessary. But in fact there is nothing necessary in the existence either of the self or of the discussion. Why should there be?

One wants to say, of course, not only that the existence of the "I" isn't logically necessary, but also that there simply is no such *thing* to exist. There is no such thing as the pure ego, the referent of "I," for so soon as one proposes some experience, some set of characteristics, some Humean "perception," as a concrete referent, then since I in turn know it, I must be different from it, and so the attempt to refer misses its mark. Therefore "I" must refer to a pure indeterminate, for the logic of referring by means of it guarantees its purity by disqualifying whatever referent comes along. And, we can be sure, there *are* no pure indeterminates.

But why be so mysterious? Aren't "I" this philosophy professor, this stockbroker, housewife, pharmacist, etc.—this well-defined person with concrete characteristics? If I know my characteristics, then I know myself. I—this *person*—am fat, fortyish, a philosopher, etc. Here we have an amended version of the Strawsonian position: what makes me myself is not the characteristics of my ego (which has no characteristics), but rather my characteristics as a person. These suffice to identify me, to give me a determinate nature (I *am* fat, fortyish, and a philosopher), and to differentiate me from other persons (not everyone is fat, fortyish, and a philosopher). However, unlike the original Strawsonian position, here these characteristics are all P-predicates. My having them implies not only that I am conscious of having them, but that others also are conscious that I have them and that I am aware that I have them. I have them, just as Henry has his weight of 150 lbs., by an implied agreement with everyone else that these are my characteristics, the grounds for such a claim as I have upon the attention and deference of others. My identity is in this sense my social identity, or, as we sometimes say, my social role.

A social role, however, is too impermanent and too dependent upon others to be confused with what we call "personal identity." One isn't born having a social role, one learns to have one, and what one has changes as one ages. And a role-identity demands other's cooperation, which might not be forthcoming. I can be a stockbroker only if they are willing to be fellow brokers, customers, SEC officials, etc., with respect to me. If they cease to play these roles with respect to me—after my conviction for fraud, say—I don't disappear, but I take on another identity, another role. Accordingly, I wasn't this stockbroker—the role was an accident, not my essence. I must be—indeterminate? But we rejected that!

And yet finding out what "I" refers to is, so to speak, the Name of the Game. It is what the philosophy of mind is all about. Hence we cannot run away from the pure ego as if it were an embarrassment. To dismiss the topic with the familiar quotes from Hume and Kant is mere dogmatism. We simply have the problem that "I" must have a referent, and yet cannot have one.

But why is that the problem and not also the solution? Do I have an identity, a role, a set of characteristics, the way a stone has a weight? "The stone weighs 150 lbs." means all observers agree that it has that weight. The stone itself has nothing to do with bringing about this agreement: it persists in its stupid silence while we argue about it, heave it up onto the balance, weigh it, and proclaim the result. "Henry weighs 150 lbs.," like "Henry is a stockbroker," is a different affair entirely: it is a proposition observers can agree upon only if Henry agrees too, and puts a great deal of effort into bringing about their agreement; otherwise the proposition will lack a subject. What I am is not something determinately characterized, but the activity of characteriz-

ing myself, of role-playing, of conferring upon myself a social identity. Since the identity I seek is a social identity, an
identity-as-over-against-others, success in the pursuit of it
depends as much on others as on myself. Indeed, this activity
cannot cease with any given success. I cannot be or be thought
by others to be totally dependent on any given identity; if
I were, I should be too fragile a thing to stand over against
them, for if they withdrew their approval, I should be left
without a self, and that is a fate which, as a matter of logic,
I cannot actively seek.[5]

The ego therefore is neither determinate or indeterminate.
It *is* the activity of determining itself. It hovers between "is"
and "isn't" in the way any process hovers between "is" and
"isn't." Surely this is an embarrassment only to those who
assume that nothing can really *be* except what has the
changeless, perdurable existence of micro-particles. And
that is not philosophy, but a theological prejudice.

5) The Body In and Out of the Laboratory.

If one looks for predicates which naturally differentiate
persons from one another, predicates, in other words, which
have some status in the natural sciences; or, which comes
to the same, if one looks for predicates which naturally differentiate persons from things (as one does when working
with the problems raised by robots), then one is looking in
the wrong place for the wrong item. Since persons make
themselves different from one another and from things, the
resulting differences, as signs or tokens of this activity, will
be conventional, not natural, or made, not given. To say this
is to say that a person cannot "have" a body the way a stone
"has" a cubical shape or a weight of 150 lbs. Instead, per-

[5] I have argued this point at some length in "The Genesis of Privacy." (Cf. fn. 2.).

sons must indicate to one another their differences from one another, and therefore they make use of the materials at hand for doing so, of which the most fundamental are their bodies. In other words, persons don't find themselves located in space and time *and then* interact with one another; rather, persons locate themselves in space and time *by* interacting with one another.

If one assumes that nature is that of which natural scientists give accounts to one another, that about which scientists construct proofs intended to convince one another, then surely the differences between scientists must be logically prior to whatever information they may pass about among themselves—for were it not for these differences, the information would not need to be passed about. Therefore the device by which a scientist communicates to his colleagues that he is a fellow investigator to whom proofs are owed and from whom proofs may be anticipated—I mean his body—cannot be something whose status the course of inquiry can alter or diminish. If scientists did not know themselves to differ from one another, then they would not know how to communicate proofs to one another. The content of the proofs communicated cannot deny or distort what the scientist knows about these differences, since the differences are what the proofs, as ways of communicating, are defined by or are functional with respect to. Accordingly the body is first of all a conventional symbol, and only afterward part of the furniture of the natural world.

Said in still a third way, we noted earlier that persons have a function in language different from that of things: we talk about persons, but we also talk *to* them. We say that the properties a thing has really are the properties it has objectively, or for everybody; and we say that the most refined techniques for achieving this objectivity are those we employ in the natural sciences. But even in the laboratory amid (we may suppose) the clutter of sophisticated instruments, isn't the operational meaning of "for everybody" determined in the end by the commonplace little dramas through which we apprehend one another's bodies? "The sample is red," I say, looking through the microscope. I mean the sample is red for everybody, but that means I know what it would mean for somebody else—you, for example—to look at it. And that means I know how to get my head out of your way, how to step aside to let you look, not assaulting you, not distracting you by shouting in your ear, etc. In other words, I know how to let you have your body over there while I have mine over here, and you know that I know this, for we have tacitly agreed to treat one another's bodies as ceremonial objects and to abide by a common code of etiquette.[6] Thus we have to take for granted the meaning of the body as a courtesy object in order to define the objectivity which in turn defines the sciences.

The traditional mind-body problem arises when we ask how we get from currents in the synapses and the like to ideas, sensations, in general first-person experiences or mental events. In order to talk about currents in the synapses, C-fibers, etc., we must define the human body as a physical object whose functioning is most accurately tested in the laboratory, and we have to say that the most authoritative account of how the human body is put together is the physiologist's account. But the human body must have already been defined as an object of social ceremony, as something existing in a social situation, before the physiologist can have something to account for. "He gives the authoritative account." Yes, but of what? The problem is how to pass from

[6] The best discussion of this point is that of Erving Goffman, "The Nature of Deference and Demeanor," *American Anthropologist*, Vol. 58 (June, 1956), pp. 473–502; reprinted as No. 97 in the *Bobbs-Merrill Reprint Series in the Social Sciences.*

a certain laboratory object (or laboratory account of an object, if you prefer) to ideas, sensations, etc. But the laboratory object is an abstraction from something which we know in advance has ideas, sensations, etc., or we wouldn't have called it "human." It doesn't have those ideas, sensations, etc. in the physiology laboratory, but instead in social situations in everyday life. The laboratory is too lean an environment, too impoverished a test condition.

Chlorine, for example, is relatively simple stuff. A chlorine atom behaves the same on the dinner table as in the laboratory or on the surface of the sun. A rat, similarly, is a comparatively simple animal, and one can create in the laboratory situations which test every capacity the rat has. We cannot duplicate everyday life in the laboratory, however, for the logical reason that the laboratory itself is part of everyday life. Accordingly, the laboratory situation has to be an abstraction, an impoverishment, just because it is only a part. In everyday life, everything we know about a person, our total reaction to him in the social situation, determines how we take and what we take to be his inner experience, his ideas, sensations, etc. There is no *metaphysical* problem about passing from information about his body to information about his mind: the two are continuous with one another in the situation. His body is precisely what can express whatever he has on his mind, and his mind is precisely what can use that body to express itself. Both propositions are tautologies.

If, however, we take the body out of its natural habitat—the everyday social situation—and abstract away most of what is significant about it, reduce it to the least common denominator of the physiology laboratory, then if we can't pass from *this* account of the body to ideas, sensations, inner experiences, why is there a mystery, a metaphysical problem? If you leave out most of the information about the body which in everyday life enables you to understand what others have on their minds, then if you cannot understand how the residue can have an accessible mind, it must be because you have forgotten your own act of abstraction. Everyday social life is the natural habitat of man. He cannot display what is most characteristic of him—thought—in a leaner environment. Why is this mysterious?

6) Inside the Great Leviathan: The Group Mind.

Toward the end of his argument, Strawson entertains the fantasy of "a special kind of social world in which the concept of an individual person has no employment, whereas the analogous concept for groups does have employment" (150). In such a world, where the members of groups think, feel, and act as one, it would be natural to individuate the members as organic bodies, but to credit nothing smaller than the group itself with a mind. Thus in such a world, the subject of M-predicates would be the body of the individual member, while the subject of P-predicates would be the group itself. Our concept of a person would not be applicable, for its applicability requires that the subjects of these two kinds of predicates must coincide. In fact, Strawson maintains, ". . . we ourselves, over a part of our social lives —not, I am thankful to say, a very large part—do operate conceptual schemes in which the idea of the individual person has no place, in which its place is taken, so to speak, by that of a group. . . . The point I wish to make is that a condition for the existence, the use, of the concept of an individual person is that this should happen *only sometimes*" (151).

If, however, M-predicates cannot bear the individuating burden Strawson imposes on them, if, in other words, the body gains its significance as a symbol of individuation by being taken up in the process by which persons individuate themselves from one another, then it follows that the distinction between an individual mind and a group mind cannot

be drawn as Strawson draws it—as if the two were alterna-
tives at the same logical level, as if it were a question which
of the two has use, applicability, or employment, as if minds
and bodies came in the same sized packets by a strange pre-
established harmony. If by a "group mind," Strawson means
a process of communication which creates the communicants,
in which the individual comes to be himself, one individual
among many, because the group governs his thoughts and
actions, then we may say that over all of our social lives
—and that means over all of our lives—we think and act as if
we were parts or members of a group mind. "There is no
sense in speaking of the individual consciousness just as
such: for there is no way of identifying such pure entities"
(151). Therefore in order to be an individual subject of experience, one must concretely differentiate oneself from other individual subjects of experience. But since no party to
this transaction is an individual subject until he has differentiated himself from others, the transaction cannot be
unilateral. It must be a collective action by which both society and its members come into being. The function of the
role metaphor is to help clarify this very reciprocity or mu-
tuality.

The result of the socialization process is society and its
members. The process is teleological: it may be said to aim
at this result. We as philosophers are able hypothetically
to recapture the process, to describe how it must work, for
it doesn't always work. We learn about it from its failures
and misfires and from their fate at our hands. We learn
how persons are required to manage their bodies by study-
ing the forms of mismanagement which will disqualify them
as persons.

Of course, Society—that great leviathan—is only a mor-
tal god. Our collective efforts are as liable to failure as our
individual ones. This may seem a dismaying thought. One
wants others to be as apodictically certain of one's self-

consciousness as one is oneself. This, surely, is the source of the philosophical concept of individual autonomy. If the socialization process is to set up individuals as autonomous units, a considerable mobilization of effort is required. The body can be made to perform its symbolic function only by being wrenched and twisted from its natural course, its rhythms interrupted, its shape distorted, its drives repressed. Autonomy must be made to seem preeminently desirable to the individual, so desirable, in fact, that he takes it to be a logical fact, a fact whose opposite is unthinkable. And, in a sense, it is unthinkable—in the sense, namely, that if he is to enjoy the privilege of thinking for himself, of privately knowing his own self-contained and self-sustaining substantiality, then the socialization process must succeed. To take comfort from this, however, is to take comfort from a tautology.

The fact that to disguise the teleological moment here, to represent one's autonomy to oneself as if it were a permanently affixed state, like the shape of a stone, is a falsification, is well enough attested by Strawson, who is "thankful to say" that, over the largest part of our social lives, we do not need to pay attention to the elaborate group labor which makes possible individual self-consciousness. For the most part, we can enjoy the play and ignore the stage-machinery. The success with which philosophers celebrate their own autonomy by ignoring the process is the best possible proof that it usually works. On the other hand, I argue that it doesn't have to work, and that to recognize one's dependence on the joint ceremonial efforts of all is not to forego one's autonomy, but to know it for what it is. That this position is morally sounder follows from the fact that the fulfillment of an obligation to be autonomous depends upon one's recognition that it is a task to be performed, not a fact to be rather sentimentally described.

In summary, I assume that our "common human nature" (150) is our social nature. If there is to be such a thing as society, then there must be individual members of society. If there are to be individuals then those individuals must be able to make known to one another at once their common human nature ("I am like you") and their individual differences ("I am like you in that I don't have to agree to whatever you say just because you say it, but you have to persuade me"). The last formulation is intended to suggest that in fact these two moments imply one another: what each person abstractly has in common with each other person is a set of concrete ways of differing from him. The mutual acknowledgment of their differences, then, is how two persons realize their common human nature.

In the end, persons have no other means for symbolizing to one another their differences from one another except their bodies, and to work the body up into a social artifact, its natural processes have to be controlled. If you wish, you may call this its "conventionalization." If the body were not conventionalized, there would be no way of determining that it is the body of a person, rather than just another natural thing. Therefore persons have to be permitted to differentiate themselves from their bodies (as their bodies' controllers), for otherwise they would have no way to differentiate themselves from one another. (One may question, then, whether the strong version of the Identity Theory[7] is a meaningful hypothesis, for to think it meaningful is to envisage a social situation in which persons no longer have the ability to differentiate themselves from their bodies, which contradicts what we mean by a person).

A natural object has characteristics for the persons who

---

[7] For the strong version—weak version distinction, see Richard Rorty, "Mind-Body Identity, Privacy, and Categories," *Review of Metaphysics*, Vol. XIX, No. 1 (September, 1965), pp. 25–28.

know it, but not for itself. In other words, it has M-predicates but no P-predicates. Persons, on the contrary, have M-predicates only by having P-predicates. This is most accurately viewed as a subtle and important tautology. Persons entitle one another to have characteristics (and so to differ) by acknowledging one another's characteristics, transforming them into what might be called "biographical material." Therefore what is stuck by others with a characteristic the way a stone is stuck with its shape or its weight is not a person. To have a characteristic as persons have characteristics—let it be a grotesque nose—is to be allowed to play the role of One Who Knows He Has A Grotesque Appearance And Modifies His Behavior Accordingly—actually not a role, but a class of roles. He may be tragically gallant like Cyrano, he may revel in his wicked rejection of his rejectors like the Penguin, etc. Now it is tautological to say that if someone has an M-predicate (the nose), then it is entirely up to him to decide how he shall convert that M-predicate into a P-predicate (biographical material), for those and only those things which are permitted this initiative—this privacy! —are persons. Therefore it is obviously possible to collapse something into a collection of M-predicates, but it is not possible to do so while at the same time treating it (favorably *or* abusively) as a person. "Are you now seeing a red patch (feeling a pain, etc.) or aren't you?" I cannot know until you tell me, but only because I cannot know who you are (what role you are playing) until you tell me. But I am not debarred from this knowledge by the opacity of your skin, but by the use you have to make and I have to permit you to make of your body in order to be a person. But I cannot be a person myself unless I permit you to differ from me; therefore I must allow you your characteristics, and so your privacy as well.

Index